New Patterns for Discipling Hindus

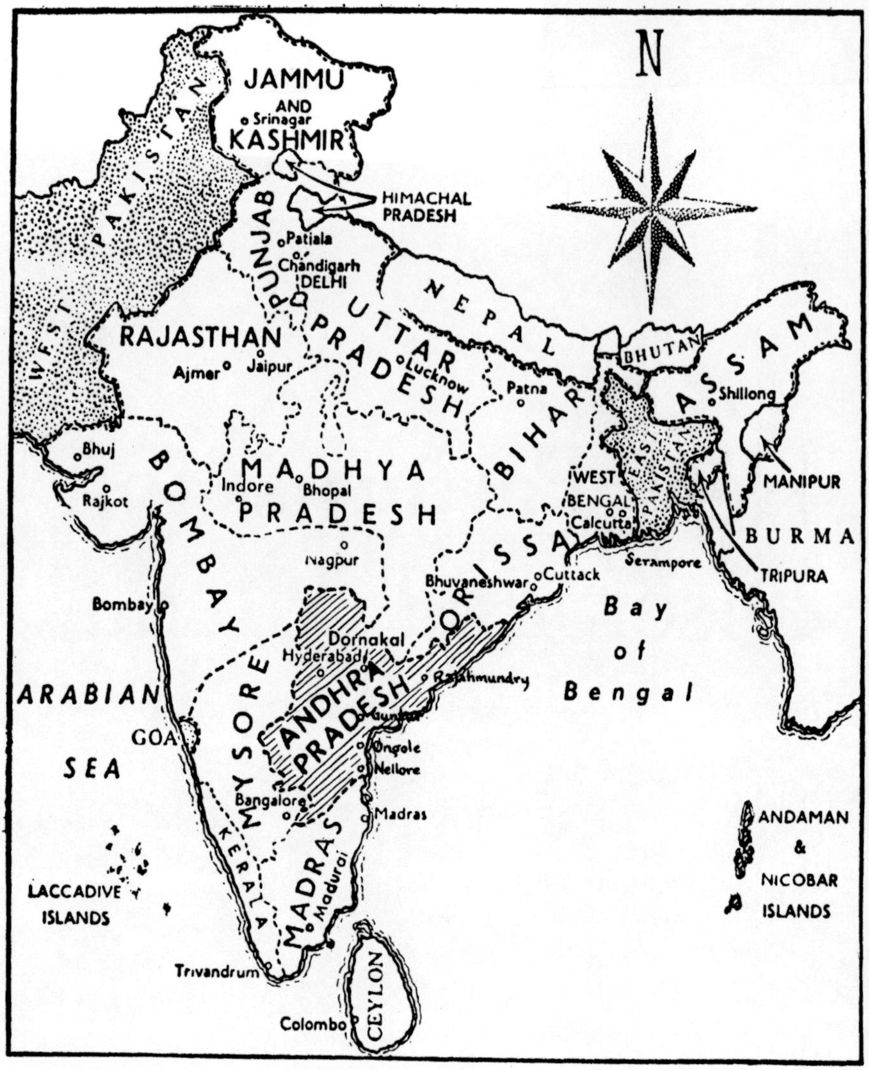

INDEPENDENT INDIA

Showing State Boundaries

as Revised along Linguistic Lines in 1956

New Patterns for Discipling Hindus

The Next Step in Andhra Pradesh, India

B. V. Subbamma

William Carey Library
Pasadena, California

International Standard Book Number: 0-87808-306-5
Library of Congress Catalog Number: 76-128755

Published by *William Carey Library*
P.O. Box 40129
Pasadena, CA 91114
U.S.A.

PRINTED IN THE UNITED STATES OF AMERICA

To My Mother

CONTENTS

PREFACE 1

Chapter

I ANDHRA PRADESH, THE LAND AND PEOPLE 3
- Language: Telugu 4
- Social Structure 5
- Caste Today 6

II THE PROTESTANT CHURCHES IN ANDHRA PRADESH 13
- The Church of South India 13
- Baptist Churches of the Northern Circars 16
- Andhra Evangelical Lutheran Church 18
- Samavesam of Telugu Baptist Churches 20
- South Andhra Lutheran Church 22

III HOW THE PROBLEM AROSE 25
- My Conversion Experience 25
- How the Problem Looked to Dr Pickett 33
- How the Problem Looked to Me 37
- How the Problem Looked to Rev. S. W. Schmitthenner 42

IV THE CRUCIAL PROBLEM IN DISCIPLING HINDUS 52
- Can They Become Christians in Their Own Culture? 52

Should They Necessarily Become the Members of the Existing Church? 60
Should They Necessarily Become the Members of Another Homogeneous Unit? 67
The Advantage of Separate Congregations 77
The Note of Urgency for the Establishment of Congregations Among Hindus 94

V NEW PATTERNS OF CHURCH GROWTH 100
Five Theological and Methodological Considerations 100
The People Movement Concept Applied to Hindu Ethnic Units 107
Communication Theory Urges Recognition of Social Strata 109
Indigenous Church Principles Demand Freedom of Each People to Follow Its Own Culture 110
Fitting Worship to the Converts 111
New Patterns of Church Growth Involve New Ways of Evangelism 112
Modern Methods of Communication 118
Urban Church Planting 119

VI NEW PATTERNS OF LEADERSHIP 125
Church Leaders on the Effectiveness of Pastors and Workers from the Caste Background 125
New Structures Demand New Patterns of Leadership 127
Theological Education 132
Theological Education by Extension 138

VII THE NEW ROLE OF MISSIONS TODAY IN ANDHRA 144
The Need for the Missions 144
The Duties of Mission in Pioneer Church Planting 147
Specific Opportunity for the Board of World Missions

of the Lutheran Church in America 148
The Continuing Responsibility of the Existing Church 149

VIII RECOMMENDATIONS 151
1. Research Project in Andhra Pradesh 151
2. Training Five Kinds of Leaders 151
3. Church Growth Through Theological Education 153
4. Theological Education by Extension 154
5. Establishment of House Churches Among Converts 155
6. Ordination for Different Levels of Preachers 156
7. Ordination for Women 157
8. An Order for Women 158
9. New Methods of Evangelism 159
10. Ashram Programmes 160
11. Scripture Distribution 161
12. Outreach Through the Institutions 162
13. Indigenous Worship 162
14. Indigenous Literature 162
15. Cultural Heritage 163
16. The Church's Responsibility to Evangelize Harijans and Other Hindus 164
17. Board of World Missions Implements the Programme of New Approach to Hindus 165

CONCLUSION 166

APPENDICES 167
Appendix A. Questionnaire 167
Appendix B. Questionnaire 168
Appendix C. Questionnaire 169
Appendix D. Proposed Research Project in Andhra Pradesh 170
Appendix E. The Joint Family 173

BIBLIOGRAPHY 175

FOREWORD

Bold new solutions for vexing problems facing the Church are really both promising and biblically permissible; but Miss Subbamma's proposal is both.

The problem, to which she addresses herself, is beyond question vexing. In India the caste system, for three thousand years legalized and by the Hindu religion sanctified, still greatly influences all life in that populous sub-continent. Though "untouchability" has been declared unconstitutional, like America, India has found that race prejudice (communal feeling it is called) persists in the hearts of men. Though interdining between the highly educated of various communities (castes) is now common, it is still rare among the orthodox masses. Intermarriages are counted at the very top by the hundreds while marriages within one's own community number millions. Caste remains vivid and influential. How does all this affect the Church with its ten or twelve million Christians?

"The vast majority of Christians in India," to quote Bishop Neill, "are of depressed class or animistic origin." Most Christians are landless laborers. Therefore, despite some hundreds of thousands of Christians descended from caste converts, the middle and upper castes in India regard Christianity as an "untouchable religion." To become Christian is to become one with the Harijans. Christians, of course, vigorously deny that Christianity is a serf religion. Educated Hindus who have travelled abroad and are citizens of the 'one world' know very well that Christianity is a world religion which has its fair share of the wise and powerful of earth; but most people are not influenced by the 'one world.' Their locality forms their world and in their village, their city, and their province, Christians are very lowly people indeed. To become Christian is precisely to leave one's own people, one's natural caste, and join the lowest of low communities. Under these circumstances, the Christian faith, despite great efforts, grows very slowly. Christ is admired and loved, but since baptism and the consequent interdining and intermarriage lead men away from their own "folk," caste people seldom 'become Christians.'

Facing this very difficult problem, a few theologians sound as if they were encouraging caste people to become--not Christians, for the word is despised--but Hindu Christians, without baptism, without an authoritative Bible, without the Church, and without the Lord's Supper. The 'solution' is neither biblically permissible nor promising. Most Christian leaders in India facing this problem, therefore, resign themselves to centuries of no growth, during which--they hope--the Christians will somehow rise to middle class standing. A few leaders have actually proposed that the Churches stop baptizing the lowly and lift a few at least of the existing Christians through education to middle class position, thus letting Christianity be seen as 'respectable.'

The problem is so keen that in most provinces in India the Sudhra, Vaisya, Kshatriya and Brahmin castes are either actively indifferent or hostile to the Christian faith. However, in Andhra Province where hundreds of thousands of the lowest of the low became Christians between 1870 and 1970, the middle castes---seeing the indigenous forms of Christianity all about them---have begun to turn responsive to the Gospel. Some thousands of Reddys, Kammas, Kapus, Lambadis, and others have, as individuals or small groups, taken the tremendous leap of faith and become Christians. They worship with existing Christians in church houses which in villages and small towns are built in the palems---outside ghettos.

While these caste converts are highly to be commended, it is proving difficult for them to bring others of their fellow castemen into the Church. Many Hindu women have become baptized Christians, but their husbands will not be baptized, hence their children reared as Hindus are married back into their own community, usually to non-Christians.

Miss Subbamma is one of these middle caste converts, who paid the tremendous price of complete identification with the existing Church made up of Harijan Christians--though revulsion against caste is so great in the Churches that the phrase 'Harijan Christian' is strictly taboo. For more than twenty years she has carried on women's evangelistic work in Andhra Province. She knows the people of every community. As principal of a Women's Training Centre, she has trained hundreds of the finest girls of the Christian community and is held in respect and affection by leaders of the Churches, not only Lutheran but Baptist and C.S.I.

In this wide ranging book she sets forth a bold new plan for winning caste people to joyful, liberating discipleship to Jesus Christ. Her plan is biblically sound---she strongly advocates open confession of Christ, public baptism with water, celebration of the sacraments, and fellowship with the One Church. She is theologically literate, having her Bachelor of Divinity from famed Serampore. She is well aware of the theological and ecclesiological dimensions of the situation. She is a loyal Lutheran and expects converts from Hinduism in her parts of the province to belong to Lutheran churches, and in other parts of the province (where Baptists or Church of South India are strong) to belong to congregations of those Churches.

Miss Subbamma is a woman of wide sympathies and experience. She quotes approvingly from Bishop Newbigin, Bishop Neill, Dr. D. T. Niles and other leaders of the World Council of Churches. She also draws on the wisdom of leaders of the more conservative Evangelical wing of the Church.

I commend this book to all readers. As they peruse it, they will see an outline of things to come, the patterns according to which the great castes of India, and peoples of other lands too, will in the years ahead come to Christian faith and bring the riches of their culture to be blessed and multipled by Him whose they rightfully are.

Donald McGavran, Dean
School of World Mission
Fuller Theological Seminary

PREFACE

The Board of World Missions of the Lutheran Church in America has given me the opportunity to study in the School of World Mission of the Fuller Theological Seminary. The purpose of this year of study was to enable me to devise a really effective "Christian Approach to Hindus." The Long Range Planning Committee of our Lutheran Church has asked me to present a considered statement of this approach to the Church and to the Board of World Missions.

The burden to evangelize Hindus came to me at my baptism and has rested on me from the time that I became a Christian. I have long felt the desire to work out a solution for the many seemingly unnecessary problems which prevent non-Christians from becoming disciples of Christ. This thesis analyzes the situation and suggests solutions.

Today, Hindus are more responsive than ever before. But the growth of the Church among them is nevertheless regrettably small. The problem is complex. Among other things, Hindus want to become Christians in their own culture and to worship in their own localities.

New patterns of church growth need new leadership and a new role for Missions. There is great urgency to start new patterns of evangelism among Hindus. The doors are opened for communicating the Gospel and churches must be planted among these receptive homogeneous groups before the doors are closed---and doors are closing in many parts of the inhabited world.

Method of Procedure

My conversion experience and my work among the Hindus over ten years has provided me with many insights. The study (1933) of Dr. J. W. Pickett regarding the middle-class Hindus in Andhra, and the thorough case study done by the Rev. S. W. Schmitthenner in 1968 concerning our Lutheran evangelizing among Sudhras, presented a clear picture of the successes and failures in the method of approach to the discipling of non-Christians.

My own experience with an Ashram programme during 1968-1969 helped me to understand the growing responsiveness of the men and women of the different non-Christian societies. Over 500 people heard the Gospel at our Ashram, through which we reached thousands in many villages.

Reading many books in the "Church Growth Series" and my study in the many courses of the School of Missions have stimulated my thinking. Questionnaires, and interviews and correspondence with experts have all enlightened me.

Acknowledgements

I am highly indebted to my major professor, Dr. Donald McGavran, who has been a great source of information and inspiration to me as I wrote this thesis. He has generously given of his time to discuss the whole complex situation, and also its many social and theological issues, and has patiently edited the manuscript.

I am grateful to the members of the faculty for many helpful interviews. I express my special thanks to the president of our Lutheran Church, the Rev. S. W. Schmitthenner, for the valuable material received from him. The interest of Dr. John Mangum and Dr. J. F. Neudoerffer in the cause of promoting the Gospel among Hindus has been a great encouragement to me. I am grateful to them and to the Board of World Missions of the Lutheran Church in America, for the valuable study at the School of World Mission and Institute of Church Growth. I want to thank our Church for granting me study leave. My thanks are also due to Mrs. Evans for her excellent typing.

1

Andhra Pradesh The Land and People

The Union of India occupies the major portion of the Indian subcontinent---a vast three-cornered peninsula in South East Asia. Since November, 1960, India has been divided into six territories administered by the central government and fourteen states. The fourteen states (with their estimated population) are shown in the map. Andhra Pradesh is on the south-eastern flank of India, shaped like a plough share--in size, the fifth biggest state in India, and in population, the fourth biggest, spreading over 106,053 square miles. It is one of India's riverine areas with thirty-four rivers, the biggest being the Godavari and the Krishna. It consists of twenty districts divided into 185 taluks and the capital is located in the city of Hyderabad. Andhra Pradesh possesses a variety of geological formations and the soils can be broadly divided into six types. This is a surplus state in agricultural production, growing 98 percent of India's Virginia tobacco.

The people are hard-working and intelligent. About 67 per cent of Andhra people are cultivators. The principal farming communities of the state are the Kammas, Reddys, Kapus, Velamas, Rajus, Gavaras and Gollas.

> Their distinguishing trait is sincerity and boldness and they express their views with a refreshing frankness. Like most farmers of India, they are generous in their hospitality. (Raghavan 1961:195)

The total normal area sown in Andhra Pradesh is 29,098,210 acres of which 22,285,210 acres are under food crops. Rice is the state's staple crop and mango is its prize fruit. The farmers are progressive in outlook and are fertilizer-minded.

Cattle raising is most important for them. A Telugu proverb says: "If there is no pasture there are no cattle; without cattle there is no manure; and without manure there is no harvest." (Raghavan 1961:183) This proverb sums up the farmer's attitude towards his livestock.

The Kammas, the Reddys, and the Kapus are the dominant castes in many villages of Andhra. They own a large portion of the land and many are prosperous. The Kammas are in a majority in Krishna and Guntur districts. They are a fine farming community. Women also work in the fields and they obtain a place of honour in the family. Reddys are big land owners and there are several subdivisions among them. Kapus constitute an important section of the cultivating class. They are in great numbers in East and West Godavari districts and groups of them have settled in the Rayalaseema, Medak, Hyderabad and Nizambad districts of Telangana.

Among the above mentioned communities in recent years, education has spread greatly. Many have become lawyers, engineers, doctors, and educationists. Large numbers of women are in professions of education and medicine. Most leading politicians are from the Kammas and the Reddys, many of whom hold government posts. They also hold hereditary posts as village headmen and munsiffs.

Up to recently, these middle castes have been of little importance in the spread of the Gospel. However, as the rest of this thesis will show, their importance has rapidly grown in this respect, as well as socially.

A most important section of the population, especially from the viewpoint of the past propagation of the Gospel, has been that of landless labourers. These are commonly called the Harijans.

Language: Telugu

This language spoken by over fifty million people and, having a rich literature, is considered to be very melodious.

The Telugu script comes from ancient Sanskrit, which is equally the source for all modern Indian scripts. By the thirteenth century, it had become distinct from other Southern scripts and assumed its present form.

Warneck, a recognized authority, is quoted as saying:

> The modern Telugu character may fairly claim to be the most beautiful and the most convenient of all the Indian characters. It has a great fondness for rounded forms, derived from the habit of writing with the stylus on palm leaves, on which straight lines and angles could hardly be made without splitting the leaf. Every consonant has its vowel attached, so that each character really represents a syllable. The characters are very clear, and capable, unlike those of Hindustani, of being easily printed. Even when writing rapidly by hand, they are far more legible than is generally the case with the Indian languages. (Dolbeer 1959:33)

All the Telugu-speaking people are called Telugus or Andhras, regardless of former boundaries.

Social Structure

Long ago Hinduism divided Indian society into four big groups or castes: the Brahmins, or priests and scholars; the Kshatriyas, or warriors; the Vaisyas or businessmen, artisans and farmers; and the Sudhras. In addition to the above, the untouchables or "scheduled classes" were regarded as the lowest community. Its members could not go into the market places or into the temples for worship. Their residential area was located outside the village. The mention of Dr. Ambedkar's experience would further explain the situation of the untouchables:

> Ten years in the West had blurred his memory of the workings of the caste system, and he went back to Baroda expecting a government post, but found he could not rent rooms of a house because he was an outcaste! 'I tell you I wept bitter tears,' he says, 'on the day I was hounded from place to place in Baroda, and even the memory of my days in Baroda fills my eyes with tears.' (Phillips-Godfrey, 1936:10)

The division of the village into a number of castes constitutes one of the most fundamental features of its social structure. In Hindu society, caste divisions play an important part both in actual social interactions and in the ideal scheme of values. The individual's position in the caste structure is fixed by birth, and is to this extent, immutable. The caste system gives to Hindu society a segmentary character.

The joint family has long been the common form of family organization in India, as well as in Andhra. The property of all is held in common under the trusteeship of the senior male; every male child is entitled to a share of the joint family property. All the members are fed from a single kitchen and receive money from the family purse. In recent years, the regular tendency is toward smaller joint families and in general we see many changes in family patterns.

Caste Today

Mr. Gandhi made the most outstanding effort for the removal of untouchability. He called untouchables Harijans, or "Children of God." In 1933, Mr. Gandhi openly risked his life by a twenty-one days' fast definitely undertaken to help the Harijans' cause. Under his influence, modern India has abolished all legal restrictions against its 50,000,000 untouchables. "Untouchability, the age old scourge of India, was abolished and its practice in any form forbidden." (Lutheran Vedaprakash, 1964:2)

On August 15, 1947, India attained freedom. The preamble of the constitution of India is significant to every member of that nation. It begins as follows:

> We, the people of India, having strongly resolved to constitute India into a Sovereign Democratic republic and to secure to all its citizens
>
> Justice, social, economic, political;
> Liberty of thought, expression, belief
> faith and worship;
> Equality of status and of opportunity;
> and to promote among them all.
> Fraternity assuring the dignity of the
> individual and unity of the Nation;

> in our constituent Assembly do hereby adopt, enact and give to ourselves this Constitution.

In a way, political and social barriers have fallen down. Solid social structure has crumbled. Let us examine the forces behind these great changes. Doctor A. Aiyappan (1965:8), a Hindu and an anthropologist, made the following statement:

> The political historian would describe the changes as due to governmental action, but the social legislation against untouchability, the temple entry act, and the tenancy acts were the culmination of a long process which really started with the beginnings of Westernization of India and the impact of protestant Christianity.

Thus at first glance, since the current Indian constitution strictly forbids any discrimination on the basis of caste, one might suppose that caste had ceased to be a force or had greatly diminished in power. But the truth is that the caste is still strong in India. As Professor Srinivas and others have observed, it plays a powerful part in politics and controls many other areas of life as well. A long time may pass before it disappears. The power of caste in society as a whole must be recognized and understood by those who seek to extend the Kingdom of God.

J. H. Hutton (1963:2), the former census commissioner of India and an eminent anthropologist says:

> Each caste is a social unit in itself . . . persons of one caste do not marry those of another. The extent to which a person of one caste will eat or drink with those of another is strictly limited by unwritten laws and anybody knows who is affected by them. Even a change of religion does not destroy the caste system, for Muslims, who do not recognize it as valid, are often found to observe it in practice, and there are many Muslim castes as well as Hindu; and when some reforming body breaks away from Hinduism and repudiates caste, it becomes something very like a new caste of its own. Jews and Christians also in India often form castes or bodies analogous to caste.

Many writers and anthropologists have made significant statements on caste, among them Taya Zinkin (1961:10):

> The groom may come from anywhere in India, as long as he belongs to the right caste. A Kashmiri Brahmin from Madras can marry a Kashmiri Brahmin from Assam, a merchant from Bombay can marry a merchant from Calcutta, and a Rajput from Jaipur thinks nothing of marrying into Nepal, as long as he is marrying a Rajput.

Even among the subcultures, caste feeling is predominant. Each unit is particular to maintain its solidarity. Adrian C. Mayer (1960:3) says:

> Caste membership is still pivotal in the actions of Indian villages; its commitants are so persuasive that their consideration encompasses a discussion of all major group activities. This is shown in the way I can discuss the political and economic sides of village life as aspects of caste differentiation, though caste may be less important in the latter than the former. Again, our analysis of kinship is at the same time largely an analysis of the internal structure of the subcaste. Caste, then, is the most important focus for an anthropological study of this peasant society.

Professor Dube (1955:95) observes:

> Hinduism as practised in the villages is a religion of prescribed rituals covering all the major crises of life ... and ritual differs in the practice of different castes.

Professor Majumdar (1962:36) put it rather more widely: "Caste provides codes of conduct and deviations from these are not generally tolerated." McKim Marriot (1960:6,8,10) states his opinion:

> And we must always remember that in a society of custom and ritual the term 'codes of conduct' and 'prescribed rituals' cover everything, not just how one prays or whether one blasphemes, but how one cooks, when one washes, to whom one talks, even how one dresses. The habits of castes differ from one another in something of the same way that conventions do; but on a much wider scale ... Caste not only governs how one lives one's life. It also fixes the place in society in which one lives it ... Caste is the way of life which

> divided society into small groups, each of which lives in a rather different way from the rest... In the long turmoil that was Indian history, caste held together the fabric of society; the integrity of the village was built round the framework of caste.

M. N. Srinivas (1960:6,9) observes:

> Caste is even today an institution of great strength, and as marriage and dining are forbidden with members of other castes, the members of a caste living in a village have many important ties with their fellow castemen living in neighbouring villages. These ties are so powerful that a few anthropologists have been led into asserting that the unity of the village is a myth and the only thing which counts is caste... Caste is an institution of prodigious strength and it is pervasive... In many spheres the strength of caste has increased in the last few decades, and bitterness between castes is a prominent feature of our urban life.

The above statements definitely indicate that the caste is a real force among different communities in India.

Let us consider what the modern Indian anthropologist, Iravati Karve of Deccan, will say regarding caste:

> In the three villages surveyed not a single marriage had occured (sic) outside the caste... only one or two people among the higher castes expressed the opinion that they did not mind mixed marriages. As many as 25 to 50 per cent of the Mahars (an untouchable caste) expressed willingness to give their daughters to touchables or receive brides from touchables, but were not willing to enter into marriage relation with Mangs, another untouchable caste. What is happening in urban and semi-urban areas can be gauged from the extract below.
>
> A Survey of marriages registered in Poona City and district during the years 1955 and 1956 showed that out of a total of 5,895 Hindu marriages 126 (2 percent (sic) were marriages between castes belonging to different caste-clusters (not necessarily to different varnas) was 41 (0.6 percent (sic) and the marriages of Hindu with people of other religions were 32. All

> the other marriages were inside the endogamous caste. From these figures one might say that marriages across the caste-cluster and varna were also as rare as marriage out of one's religion. The higher incidence of marriages within the caste-cluster called Brahmin need not be accepted as evidence of a continuation of the supposed solidarity or homogenity in the Brahmin varna. The Brahmins are the most educated caste of Maharashtra. They have been advocating social reforms and especially inter-Brahmin cluster marriages for a long time and anti-Brahmin movements of the past 50 years have made them all of a common destiny. These events in recent history can explain the higher incidence of sub-marriages. It may be noted that of the 41 marriages of people of different caste-clusters, 28 were those in which one partner was a Brahmin. This survey has been carried out by Mr. Mokashi, a student of the Deccan College, Poona.
>
> As regards inviting people to meal, going to others for a meal and visits for a few days, the activities were confined in nearly 90 per cent of cases to the kinship group. The remaining 10 per cent were within the caste group. The same was the case with friendships. Dr. McKim Marriot of the University of Chicago, in a personal observation in north Indian villages also, friendships outside the caste group were not only rare, but were generally accompanied by much shame and feelings of guilt. Gift-giving where the pattern is not disturbed by modern business relations, is confined almost purely to the kin group . . . Thus purely social activities were confined within the caste, while economic activities cut across the caste frontiers. (Iravati Karve, 1961:34)

By dealing with caste at length, I am only bringing to the notice of the reader that, whether we say it out loud or not, caste is present in Indian society, Leach also says:

> For an anthropologist in the comparison of kinship structures there is nothing that is peculiar to Indian caste. Internally, a caste presents itself to its mem-

> bers as a network of kin relationships, but this network is of no specific type. The kinship systems of caste-ordered societies vary, but all types are readily duplicated in other societies historically unconnected with the Indian world. As Morgan discovered the formal kinship organization of the Tamils (of India) is not unlike that of the League of the Iroquois. (Leach 1962: 7)

I am convinced that the great concern of Christians must be how to present the Gospel to such a society as Andhra without interfering with its culture.

Finally, I agree with Canjanam Gamaliel, an ordained Lutheran from India, when he says our

> purpose is not to defend caste but to state that caste as a social structure and an order of preservation has a role in society in India until the Gospel can transform society and create a new order of preservation. That new order is yet to evolve.

When we present the Gospel, we should not put any obstacles in the way of the inquirers to come to the Lord. To quote Mr. Gamaliel again:

> How shall we proclaim the Gospel? By condemning caste and, cudgel in hand, trying to break it and in the process completely repelling the people? Is it Christian to make breaking caste and eating from the hand of the Pariah (Harijan) a condition for baptism and discipleship? In my opinion, after years of personal observation, the answer to these two questions is "No." To answer "Yes" would be unbiblical and indefensible. (1967:100)

The Church has no right to obscure the Gospel of God's redeeming love in Christ by placing roadblocks before men, such as insistence upon immediate abandonment of caste as a prerequisite for baptism.

Men should be brought to Christ by tribes, castes, and homogeneous units. This is the people movement point of view. To get inside a tribe or caste is important for the growth of the Church. The Church can make caste a barrier and a hindrance to the propagation of the Gospel. The Church can also make caste a carrier of the Gospel. Dr. McGavran in Bridges of God (1955) has shown effectively and clearly how the bond of relationship was the bridge over which Christian faith passed. This was true in the time of the Apostles and throughout the centuries in the history of the Church on many continents. It is true today.

The chief objectionable feature of caste was the intercaste animosity and the ruthlessness with which human rights were denied.

2

The Protestant Churches in Andhra Pradesh

There are about seventeen Protestant Churches in Andhra Pradesh. There are: The Telugu Baptist Samaveshamu, Convention of Baptist Churches of Northern Circars, the Church of South India—Medak Diocese, Dornakal Diocese, Krishna-Godavari Diocese, Rayalaseema Diocese, the Andhra Evangelical Lutheran Church, the South Andhra Lutheran Church, the Methodist Church in Southern Asia, Church of India, Pakistan, Burma, and Ceylon, the Mennonite Brethren, the Salvation Army, the Seventh Day Adventists, the Pentecostal Churches, the Godavari Delta Mission, the India Mission, the Indian Christian Assemblies, and others.

In addition to the above, several other groups, small new denominations such as the Bakht Singh group and the Joshua Daniel group, are working in the state.

Now let me present very brief sketches of several of these denominations.

The Church of South India

This came into existence in 1947 when the Anglicans and Methodists and Congregationalists united. There are fifteen dioceses in the Church of South India of which only four are in Andhra Pradesh, namely Medak Diocese, Dornakal Diocese, Krishna-Godavari Diocese, and Rayalaseema Diocese.

The Krishna-Godavari Diocese is one of the largest in the Church of South India. It occupies the coastal tract between Masulipatnam and Vizagapatnam and covers the Andhra Pradesh districts of Guntur, Krishna, East Godavari and West Godavari, and Vizak town, but the whole of the Godavari delta and the major portions of East and West Godavari districts are Lutheran areas. The diocese is wholly of the Anglican tradition and is the result of the work of Church Missionary Society Telugu Mission, which was founded about the middle of the last century.

The Medak Diocese comprises the Revenue district of Hyderabad and the Revenue districts of Medak, Nizamabad, and Adilabad. Prior to the inauguration of the Church of South India, the whole diocese was part of the Hyderabad district of the Methodist Church of South India. Except for the five ex-Anglican pastorates in the city area, the diocese is wholly ex-Methodist in tradition and is being assisted by the British Methodist Missionary Society.

The Dornakal Diocese is situated between Krishna-Godavari and Medak Dioceses. It includes the government districts of Warangal, Nalgonda, Khammamett and Karimnagar and the former agency areas in East Godavari district.

The Rayalaseema Diocese came into existence in July, 1950, by the amalgamation of two dioceses formed in 1947. It comprises the districts of Kurnool, Cuddappah, and Anantapur and the major part of the Chittoor district.

In the above four dioceses, congregations number 3,443 and the baptized community is 401,143. There are only 268 presbyters (ordained ministers), but 648 paid lay workers (unordained "village pastors"). In these dioceses, there are about 715 unpaid elders. One of the chief problems is that each ordained presbyter has to be in charge of several congregations. The need for a large increase in the number of ordained clergy is obvious. In some dioceses, this problem is being tackled by giving short courses of special training to selected senior workers and ordaining them.

Evangelistic Work

In the Medak Diocese, 271 men and 19 women are in evangelistic work. Each pastorate is divided into three or four sections and every section has a supervising evangelist. Some effort is made to bring the Gospel to the Hindus.

The Rayalaseema Diocese has a Men's Evangelistic Group which consists of a presbyter, an evangelist, a harikatha expert, and a musician. Four evangelists work under the divisional chairman.

In the Dornakal Diocese, there are large numbers of Lambadies who are responsive to the Gospel. A goodly number of them were baptized; some Scripture portions were translated into their language and are being used among them. The Bishop takes much interest in the growing Church among non-Christians. Besides the regular workers, a number of voluntary workers participate in the programme.

In the Krishna Diocese, there are are many converts from a caste background. The Kammas and Kapus respond well to the Good News. The Bishop is very enthusiastic about communicating the Gospel to non-Christians. In this diocese at Vijayawada, the Andhra Christian Council arranges a big convention. People from all over Andhra Pradesh come here to listen to the Gospel and since it takes place in this diocese, thousands are benefitted. Many Christian leaders work for the success of the convention. Great opportunities for evangelism exist.

Finances

The Medak Diocese is generously assisted by the British Methodist Missionary Society through regular as well as "cushion grants." The total amount received annually is about Rs 515,000 or $64,000. The Krishna Diocese receives a grant of Rs 1,101,412 or $137,700 from overseas. The congregations contribute money for the salaries of presbyters and deacons.

The Dornakal Diocese has a total expenditure of about Rs 277,000 or $34,600, but it gets only Rs 3,000 from the Church Missionary Society.

From the point of view of literacy and economics, Rayalaseema is one of the backward dioceses. It receives Rs 264,423 or $33,000 annually from overseas.

Institutions

In the Medak Diocese, there are 7 secondary schools, 2 middle schools, 2 teacher training schools, 301 elementary schools, and 11 boarding schools. For the maintenance of these institutions, large foreign subsidiaries are needed. In this Diocese, there are 7 hospitals and 3 dispensaries.

In Rayalaseema, the Church has only 3 secondary schools; all its elementary schools have been transferred to the state government.

In the Krishna-Godavari Diocese, the Church has 3 high schools and a few middle schools, and 322 diocesan elementary schools with 758 teachers. These last provide simple education for the children of village congregations. The Diocese also has 2 hospitals.

The Dornakal Diocese has 1 college, 9 high schools, and 7 middle schools. The State has taken over all the elementary schools except 5. The diocese also has 4 hospitals and a Leprosy Home.

Baptist Churches of the Northern Circars

According to present political boundaries, the Northern Circars comprise the Krishna district, the West Godavari district, the East Godavari district, the Vizagapatnam district, and the Srikakulam district of Andhra Pradesh on the East Coast. The membership of this Baptist Convention in 1965 was 32,735, the number of Churches 151, and the (adult) baptisms 1805. The church income from India was Rs 149,574 or $18,700. The Canadian Baptist Mission Board assists this Church and supplies missionary personnel and additional funds for the extension of the Kingdom of God in the Northern Circars.

The foundation of the Baptist Churches in the Northern Circars was laid by Thomas Gabriel who was born in Masulipatnam in December, 1837, in a humble Madiga home. He became an operator in the Government Telegraph Department at Kakinada. After a deep spiritual experience of Christ, he became a member of a Baptist church. In response to Christ's command, he resigned his job and engaged himself in a preaching ministry in the Krishna and Godavari districts.

The Rev. John McLaurin and his family reached Kakinada on March 12, 1874, where they were received by Thomas Gabriel (Lone Star Jubilee: 52). The Mission had only one missionary in 1874 and only one station, but in fifty years the Canadian Baptists have sent one hundred and sixty-seven missionaries to India. In the Golden Jubilee year (1924), in twenty stations there were one hundred missionaries and over one thousand Telugu workers including the teachers in four hundred schools. At present 115 pastors and 126 Bible women are serving in this Church. Thus, the humble beginnings of the labours of Thomas Gabriel resulted in the organization of the churches now known as the Convention of the Baptist Churches of the Northern Circars.

In January, 1879, the Rev. and Mrs. A. V. Timpany came to Kakinada and took charge of the work from the McLaurins who went on furlough. In October, 1880, the English Church was organized at Kakinada. By the time the McLaurins returned, a new chapel and a girls' boarding school were built at Kakinada. On his return, Mr. McLaurin opened the Theological Seminary at Samalkot on October 2, 1882, with seventeen men and two women.

Every local Baptist church is autonomous. The self-governing independence of the local Baptist church obviously does not prevent voluntary association---usually called unions and conventions---with other Baptist churches. For instance, to encourage cooperative efforts in evangelism and administration, a Field Council was formed.

There are various democratically elected officers in all these associations; but they have no authority over any congregation however small. Thus, the local church keeps its autonomy. The minister of the local church heads it and is ex-officio member of all boards, groups, and committees within it---but without any special powers.

The officers of each church besides the pastor are elders, deacons, secretary, and treasurer. Every church has either a deacons' board or a church council which elects its own chairman. Since Baptist churches are free and independent of others, they do not enjoy complete uniformity of practice.

This Baptist Convention, through its own Board of Missions, carries on a home mission in the Aruku Valley. The Rev. J. Victor Joseph is the Field Minister of the Aruku field. The work is being carried on and supported by the convention churches and by the women's societies in the three Northern associational areas, and in the Aruku field itself. The total yearly budget for the Aruku Valley work of the Board of Missions is nearly Rs 18,107 or $2,263.

The purpose of the Canadian Baptist Mission all along has been to establish self-propagating, self-supporting, and self-governing churches.

Andhra Evangelical Lutheran Church

The Andhra Evangelical Lutheran Church owes its origin to John Christian Frederick Heyer who was born in Helmstadt, duchy of Brunswick, Germany, on July 10, 1793. He was the third child of John Henry Gottlieb and Sophie Johanna Wagener Heyer. His parents were pious Christians and brought him up in the nurture and admonition of the Lord. At the age of fourteen, he was sent to Philadelphia. He studied and worked in the United States of America in different capacities.

When the way was opened to send out the first American Lutheran foreign missionary to India, no one could be found with better preparation for this difficult and arduous task than Father Heyer.

Father Heyer landed in Colombo on March 15, 1842, after a journey of five months from America. In April, he arrived at Madras and on May 19, he set out for Nellore in an open canal boat. He was kindly received at Nellore by the American Baptist missionaries, Van Husen and Day. After he came to Bapatla from Ongole, he tied his palankeen between two palmyra palm trees, asserting that he meant to stay there to carry on mission work; but God had other plans. Collector H. Stokes, hearing that a padre had come to Bapatla, at once sent a peon with some coolies to bring him in his palky to Guntur. Father Heyer reached Guntur on Sunday, July 31, 1842, the birthday of the American Lutheran Mission in the Andhradesa.

During the period of the separate Guntur and Rajahmundry Missions, the Guntur Synod was formed in 1906, and the Rajahmundry Synod in 1920. In April 1927, the Andhra Evangelical Lutheran Church was constituted and it united the Guntur and Rajahmundry Synods and took over their responsibilities.

The Andhra Evangelical Lutheran Church was registered under the Societies Act of 1860 on April 21, 1932. Further reorganization was carried out in 1942-1944. In 1950, the Andhra Evangelical Lutheran Church was accorded recognition by the mother church.

Evangelistic work is done by five evangelistic pastors, evangelists, and Bible women. The work of the Bible women is very significant. So far, most evangelism to non-Christians has been done by full-time men evangelists and Bible women in the field.

Finances

For 1967, the total American subsidy was Rs 1,563,561 or $195,445. Out of this amount, Rs 927,463 was used for parochial and general evangelistic work, and Rs 636,098 for educational and medical work. Total Indian receipts from the parishes is only Rs 30,500 or $3,800. Compared with what the Church receives from America, the giving of the Indian Church is very small. Urgent need exists for the Lutheran Church to develop the habit of giving to the Lord.

Institutions

The Lutheran Church has 8 high schools, 3 training schools, 1 arts and science college, and 1 college for education. Seven hospitals, a sanatorium, three schools for nurses, and the public health centre at Macherla are providing a healing ministry to both Christians and non-Christians. The School for the Blind, and Industrial School and Colony of Mercy at Rajahmundry, and at Guntur, the Industrial School for Boys, are carrying on a merciful and industrial programme. In cooperation with other Lutheran Churches, the Andhra Evangelical Lutheran Church has started several new projects like the English Medium Schools at Srisailam and Guntur, the work project at Srisailam for about 2,000 Christian labourers, and the Bhadravathi diaspora work.

Samavesam of Telugu Baptist Churches

The Rev. Samuel Day, the founder of the American Baptist Mission, and his wife sailed to India on September 20, 1835. But only in February, 1840, the family moved from Madras to Nellore. Samuel Day's health soon broke down and they left Nellore early in 1846. For several years after that, not even a single missionary family lived in Nellore and the executive committee even thought of abandoning the mission. Then Lyman Jewett offered his services and the Days were able to return to India.

When the Jewetts arrived in Nellore on April 16, 1849, with Samuel Day, things were very discouraging. Though they started a few schools again, very few converts were won among the caste people to whom missionaries addressed themselves. At the annual meeting of the Society in Albany in 1853, a motion was made to give up the mission and send the missionaries to Burma where there was more hope of success. Dr. Lansing Burrows pleaded for the mission to be continued and pointing to Nellore on the missionary map, he called it "The Lone Star." Dr. Smith caught up the words and that night before he slept, wrote a little poem and read it at the meeting in the morning. It made such a profound impression that there and then a vote was taken to continue and reinforce the mission in Nellore. Still very small success attended its labours.

The Cloughs arrived in Nellore in early 1866 and resolved to preach the Gospel to the despised Malas and Madigas who until this time had been bypassed lest preaching to them offend the caste people. Wisely the Cloughs decided to address the Gospel to the "untouchables" in Ongole, fifty miles north of Nellore. They arrived in Ongole in September, 1866, and by 1876 had a Church of nearly 3,000 baptized believers.

During the famine of 1876-1878, the Rev. J. E. Clough played an active part in relief work by taking a contract from the government of Madras for a stretch of the Buckingham Canal which was then being dug between Madras and Vijayawada and thus provided his Christians with employment and food. Later, he employed their non-Christian relatives also. As a result, multitudes of depressed class people asked for baptism; but Clough, realizing that their main object might be work and wages, refused to baptize them until the famine period was over and the people had all gone back to their homes. When they continued to beg for baptism, Clough called all the inquirers together after rice planting in July, 1878, and baptized 3,536 persons in three days. That year he baptized a total of 10,000 believers. Added to the existing 3,000, the Baptists now numbered about 13,000.

In the first hundred years, twenty-seven Field Associations were formed and the parish denomination is called the Samavesam (Convention) of Telugu Baptist Churches. According to the 1966 statistics, there are 542 churches in the Samavesam and the membership is 187,636. There are 92 ordained pastors, 295 unordained pastors, 93 Bible women, and 32 missionaries working in the field. The number of baptisms in 1966 was 8,727.

The Samavesam takes a keen interest in evangelism. Most of the churches conduct summer evangelistic campaigns. Voluntary workers' institutes are conducted in a central place in every field association.

The Baptist Youth Gospel Team, consisting of about fifteen young men and women, is doing a solid piece of work. In the summer of 1965, it witnessed for our Lord at about twelve centres. The Samavesam shows great concern for the needs of the population in industrial areas. In the summer of 1967, the Gospel Team visited the following industrial areas: Warangal, Siripur-Kaghaznagar, Nagpur, and Bilhai.

Institutions

The Baptists have 9 high schools and 32 elementary and training schools in which in 1967, 324 teachers worked and 8,727 pupils were being educated.

A healing ministry is being carried on by 3 hospitals and 2 dispensaries. About 91 men and women work in these institutions. Every year about 48,425 patients are given medical aid.

Finances

The total budget for 1965 of Rs 432,272 or $54,000 was provided from the following sources. The American Baptist Foreign Mission Society gave Rs 428,572 and the institutions contributed Rs 3,700.

This budget was used as follows: for evangelism (meaning largely salary subsidy for the 387 ordained and unordained pastors) Rs 102,382; for education Rs 156,382; for medical work Rs 19,407; and the rest of the money, Rs 145,100, was spent for other items.

South Andhra Lutheran Church

South Andhra Evangelical Lutheran Church was started in the year 1865. It celebrated its centenary in 1965 on a grand scale. According to statistics of 1962, the membership of this church is 13,584 and is found in 33 parishes. There are 16 ordained pastors and 17 unordained pastors in the church. The total number of missionaries that came to serve in the Church from 1865 to 1965 is 92. Until now, 32 Indian pastors have been ordained.

The South Andhra Lutheran Church is very anxious to become self-supporting, self-propagating, and self-governing. Regarding finances, the Church undertook a twelve-year plan and this was accepted by the home board in 1958. According to this plan, the subsidy to the South Andhra Lutheran Church was to be reduced each year by one-twelfth or so of the 1958 subsidy and to be discontinued entirely in 1970. In great faith and with great courage, the Church is carrying out the plan successfully. A decision has been taken to discontinue the subsidy for the support of the pastors. To replace the paid pastors, voluntary lay workers are raised up. But even after 1970, money may be received for special projects geared to the nurture and growth of the Church. Seventy-five per cent of the amount of each year's cut in budgeted subsidy will be given to the South Andhra Lutheran Church. This Church also does a good teaching ministry and healing ministry.

For want of space, I cannot give the history of all the Protestant Churches of Andhra. However, since the rest of them fall under the same pattern, further histories are not needed. Now let us draw some conclusions:

1) Christianity remains a foreign religion in many ways. The Churches depend mostly on foreign countries for finances and personnel.

2) It is often said that "in order to establish good relations with the majority community and also to build up a strong indigenous church, the churches must take more responsibility"; but it is extremely difficult for churches made up of landless labourers of the depressed classes to "take more responsibility" and to pay the salaries of well trained presbyters and deacons.

3) As we see in the history of the Churches in Andhra Pradesh, institutions like schools, colleges, and hospitals are still considered a chief part of the Churches's mission.

4) It is a glaring fact that paid workers are the chief ones to carry on the main task of the Church, hence, professionalism is predominant in the Church. A new type of non-professional worker is needed for effective Christian witness. In Andhra, where the non-Christian population is so great, there is an urgent need to proclaim the Good News by unpaid workers who earn their living at some secular occupation. Ordained ministers might even earn their living at some thing else (i.e. tent making) as suggested by the Commission on Evangelism of the Council of Churches.

In this connection, many years ago Roland Allen challenged us to reconsider missionary methods in the light of the Early Church and to contrast the outcome of the last 150 years with St. Paul's decade of work in Greece and Asia Minor. He was able to establish and equip churches with an ordained ministry only because he selected natural leaders approved by their group, trained them briefly, and committed them to the power and sufficiency of the Holy Ghost, ordaining them within a short time after their baptism. Most of them seem to have worked as honorary presbyters. In this way, from the beginning local churches were self-supporting and self-propagating.

5) The period of great growth of the churches in Andhra Pradesh from among the Harijans is over. The people movements among the depressed classes have run their course. Further evangelism in that direction will give small return. The government is subsidizing Harijans to remain "Hindus." Harijan evangelism should not cease. Many can yet accept Christ. But Harijan evangelism must rapidly be still further supplemented by the evangelization of the caste communities. The time has come to evangelize the receptive among the caste people.

6) The existing congregations are a tremendous source of power for the Christian movement, provided they do not absorb all mission effort and subsidy. If Christian missions can continue to assist the established Harijan churches lightly while using most missionary resources of both India and America to disciple the responsive segments of the Andhra population, the financially strong Kapus, Kammas, and Reddys can now be brought to Christian faith. The next fifty years of church and mission history in Andhra Pradesh can be a great leap forward.

3

How the Problem Arose

My Conversion Experience

At the very outset, I would like to quote the following Scripture portion to give glory to the Lord Who is solely responsible for my conversion. 'It is not that you have chosen me; but it is I who have chosen you.' (St. John 15: 16a) It is a miracle that I became a Christian; as it is written in St. Luke 19: 10: 'For the Son of Man is come to seek and to save that which was lost.' The Lord Himself sought and found me.

I was born in the Kamma community in Bodipalem, Andhra Pradesh, South India. My father, Sri Bathineni Veerayya, and my mother, Srinmathi B. Seshamma, were devoted Hindus. From the time of my grand-parents, we had gurus. One of my uncles became a guru. By virtue of being born in such an environment, orthodox Hinduism was captured by my heart from infancy.

The whole of my educational career is a mystery showing, I dare hope, that even when I did not know Him, God was directing my steps. In our families, until very recently, girls were not given much education. Because of my sister's friendship with a Christian teacher, I happened to go to a mission primary school in 1933 sponsored by the United Lutheran Church in America. During that time, it was the privilege of mission schools to teach a good deal of Scripture as a part of the regular curriculum. During five years that I attended that school, I learned a good deal of the Bible. But my caste pride was a roadblock to accept its truths. Christianity for me was the religion of "the outcastes." I did not even want to touch the Christian children so I sat in a separate corner. Naturally, I was teased for my orthodoxy. Often, irritated with their abuses of my favourite gods and goddesses, I said many unreasonable things against Jesus Christ.

The Scripture knowledge I gained came in handy to misuse it. For example, I used to argue that Rama, a popular Hindu god, was superior to Jesus because of his birth in a king's family whereas Jesus did not even have a proper house in which to be born. In Eastern countries, the cattle shed is a most degrading place for the birth of a babe. All this confirmed me in my belief that Jesus was a god only for the downtrodden outcastes.

My devotion to my Hindu gods grew year by year. One special incident drove me to consider the ultimate things life, death, sin, punishment, salvation---seriously. As a small girl, I saw a picture by the name of "Savitri," a well-known character in Hindu mythology. During the show, Savitri travels through hell fire to restore to life her husband "Satyalvantha" who had recently died. The terrible scene of hell with fire and screaming people, and other horrible sights impressed me greatly. Not knowing anything about photography, I believed what I had seen was real hell. The fear of hell seized me and it did not leave me until I accepted Jesus Christ as my Saviour. (I now believed that God used this and many other incidents to save me and to call me to His service). All the way, He led me step by step.

Even as a young girl, I took religion seriously, observed fasts, and kept vigils with much struggle. I love to eat and for me to refuse all the meals on certain days was a real sacrifice. For example, on occasions like "Yekadasi," we all believed that one should fast the whole day and keep vigil the whole night. Many times I tried to keep awake propping my eye lids open. Often I did not succeed and then I cried bitterly because I was afraid that all the merit that I earned through fasting would be cancelled. I also went on pilgrimages with my mother. Once when we were in Mangalagiri, a famous place in Andhra, I fasted the whole day, fainted, and fell down in the middle of the road. After I recovered, my mother and other relatives scolded me for my stubbornness, saying that I was too young to try to do what adults do.

Going back to my studies, I finished the fourth grade. Though there was a fifth grade in that school, my folks did not plan to educate me any further and I was all set to stay at home. The headmaster and his wife, who had been very good to me, unfortunately were about to leave the village. One afternoon I went over to the school to bid them goodbye. There by accident, or God's goodness, I ran into the new headmaster, Mr. Chukka Prakasam. He questioned me as to why I was discontinuing my studies. I told him the natural thing was for girls not to study. I would not attend the school anymore especially since my beloved teachers were leaving. He pleaded with me to continue my studies, but I told him definitely that I would not consider it anymore.

Providentially, he came up with the suggestion that he himself would teach me extra English. The opportunity to learn advanced English caught my interest and I stayed there wanting to hear more. He quickly went into his house next to the school, brought a slate, and began teaching me the English alphabet. I was thrilled to be learning a new language, and I was glad to be back again in school. After school hours, I used to go to Mr. Prakasam's house and further learn English. I was usually there practically the whole day. On certain days when I fasted, I still would go for my lesson. Being a Christian, now and then Mr. Prakasam used to remark that fasting was not necessary, but I did not like his remarks. I always had the ready answer: 'you pray to your god and we pray to our god.'

All during these years, the feeling that Christianity belongs only to the Harijans (who live outside the village in the palem) crippled my inquiry into further investigation of the truth. This feeling has been and is the common experience of many a Hindu. (All efforts should be made to bring Christianity from the fringes into the village. Ways must be found to remove the overwhelming unquestioned assumption that Christianity is exclusively an outcaste religion).

Regarding my studies, while I was doing the fifth grade, Mr. Prakasam tutored me in sixth and seventh grade subjects throughout the year, and suggested that I should join the government high school at a town twelve miles away. None of my family took any interest in the matter, but my teacher and I had confidence that somehow it might be possible for me to continue my studies. The time had come for admission. When I told my parents about it, my father got very upset about the whole idea. He thought that it was a crazy idea for a girl to leave her house and go to school in a distant town. As usual, this news spread among our relatives and friends. People like my grandmother already started to teach me cooking so that I might make a prospective bride. To her great disappointment, I was turning out to be something of a rebel. I saw my future life as different from what my people were proposing.

The day finally came when I should join the school. Even the previous evening, my father strongly objected to my going. He said, "You belong to a decent family. There is no need for you to follow what a Christian teacher suggests." I was very sad, and did not know what to do. That morning, my mother woke me up early and said she herself would take me to the high school. At that time of day, my father was not in the house. We both walked that twelve miles to Pedanandipad, and I was admitted into the eighth grade in the government high school there.

Even as a Hindu girl, I realized that this was made possible by some supernatural power and was very grateful to Mr. Prakasam. (He later became one of the pastors in our Andhra Evangelical Lutheran Church).

While I was studying and living in Kamma homes in a room my mother rented for me, I continued my sacred bathing and the rest of the rituals with a great hope of 'merit.'

One morning during history class, the teacher, Mr. Kolla Hanumanthu Rao, drew our attention to the rain ritual going on in our neighbourhood. At that time, we had not had rain for a long time. To bring rain, the Hindus were pouring water on a big statue called "Pothu Raju." Our teacher's vehement condemnation of idol worship really shocked and surprised me. His words had greater effect on me because he belonged to my beloved Kamma community. (In evangelizing peoples and nations, it should be born in mind that communication is more effective among members of the same ethnic group).

I was greatly stimulated by the chance remark of Mr. Hanumanthu Rao and to add to it, the Christian Scriptures I had learned relating to idol worship came back to me—and now for the first time with real meaning.* I am sure it was the Spirit that convicted me about the sinfulness of idol worship. In a very short time, my whole outlook was completely changed. I could no longer make myself bow before any idol.

I was faced with a great problem as to whom I should worship. The following analogy appealed to me. Like the headmaster in the school, there must be one supreme god, and just as there were many assistants to help the headmaster do the different jobs in the school, there must be many assistant gods to take care of different castes and nations. These little gods I resolved to bypass. Again, it now seems clear that I had divine guidance which directed me to pray to the supreme God.

During my senior high school days, Mr. Rajagopal Ayyangar influenced me to value the Holy Bible. He was a devoted Hindu and on every Saturday observed fasting and silence, but read the Christian Scriptures. In our classes on Saturday, he gave us written work and spent that time reading the Bible. When I discovered that, I determined to read the Bible myself. It was unbelievable how my attitude toward it had changed. Until then, because Harijan Christians had introduced it to me, I had been doubtful about the greatness of the Bible. But now the same Book in the hands of a caste man captured my interest.

In passing, once again we will notice the tremendous disadvantage of associating Christianity with a particular ethnic group. The very idea often keeps persons of other ethnic groups away from the Word of God. Furthermore, the preconceived idea that one who wishes to become a Christian should necessarily join a Harijan Christian Church prevents

*In passing, let me call attention to the fact that the Word of God itself has convincing and convicting power which speaks independent of men's intentions and expectations.

caste persons from further investigation into the matter. This has been the tragic experience of tens of thousands of Indians. To remove that kind of roadblock---I firmly believe---the Lord had used these Hindu friends as instruments of His will for my redemption.

To resume my story, one day very shortly after this, I came back to my room from the school with a great desire to possess a Bible. My desire was fulfilled but, believe me, in a mysterious way. A Hindu lady whom I knew only slightly and who never knew that I was in the least interested in a Bible called me and gave me the Holy Bible, saying that her husband got it as a present from some Christians in a meeting. The reader can imagine how much I appreciated her gift. I read the precious Book with a great enthusiasm. Sometimes I went to Mr. Ayyangar for the explanation of the difficult passages.

During that time, some amazing changes took place in my heart. The name of Jesus became so precious to me that I could hardly believe it. When I first decided to pray to the supreme God, I had considered Jesus as a Harijan god---the lowest of all gods in rank. Before I knew it, however, I was praying through the name of Jesus. This happened quite unconsciously as a miracle. I was supremely happy, having the assurance that Jesus Christ had suffered for my sin and had forgiven me and blessed me with salvation.

But the question of baptism disturbed me. I was definitely not prepared to leave my own Kamma people and join some other community. At the same time I longed to be baptized since I understood one had to be baptized if he wished to be a disciple of the Lord.

Meanwhile, I completed high school. That year my father died and my maternal uncle became the very effective head of our household. He was not in favour of further education for me; but I had a strong determination to study medicine and render great service to my country and people. Fortunately, my mother was on my side, so I managed to go to Andhra Christian College in Guntur. Here again, it was a miracle that I got admission for the science group (biology, physics and chemistry). When I first asked the principal, Dr. H. H. Sipes, for the seat, he definitely told me that my marks in physics would not qualify me for admission to the science group. I explained to him that I was very particular to study medicine and if he would not admit me for that qualifying course, I would discontinue the study. That good missionary considered my case and I was glad to be in the college. There I had opportunities to attend the Scripture class conducted by Mrs. Sipes and also to go to Sunday School.

In the environment of the Christian institution, my desire for baptism increased and I had great inner struggle. It is often said that in discipling Hindus, the crux of the problem lies in baptism.*

To Hindus, for the Holy Spirit to convert a person is not objectionable and for the individual and for groups of individuals to have spiritual experience is agreeable; but joining another community is all wrong! Christianization by asking converts to join other social and ethnic groups not only causes much loss to the individual, the family, and the community but is bad for the resulting church and prevents further spread of the Christian faith.

After being convinced of the need for baptism, it is hard on the person even to postpone it, much less to ignore it. The would-be-disciple develops a guilty conscience and such tensions lead (I expect) to mental breakdowns. I myself became almost sick and ended up in Kugler hospital in Guntur, for medical treatment.

---

*This is not true for the rite of baptism itself. The water, the complete dedication to a special deity, the words---all of these are common in Hinduism. The crux of the problem lies in one significant detail only---that baptism is believed to entail leaving one community and joining another. And this it does only at the beginning of any movement to Christ. No Harijan today joining the Lutheran Church, leaves his people. Rather he joins the advance guard of his ethnic unit. But every Hindu joining the Lutheran Church apparently has to leave his own people and "become a Christian" which means not merely the rite of baptism but the abandonment of one's own culture and kindred. Ways must be found by which men may become Christians in each Indian culture and community.

While I was there for a few days, I decided to join the Church at any cost. Right from there I wrote to the principal all about myself and my desire for baptism. After I came out of the hospital, I contacted the dean of women, a lady missionary, Miss H. Naugle. She entrusted me to an Indian pastor, Rev. Y. Aaron. He made arrangements to baptize me in Guntur but the college authorities objected since I was still a minor. Of course, all my family and relatives were terribly upset; some of them came and pleaded with me not to identify myself with the Harijans. They did not have any objection for my believing in the Lord, but they could not see me leaving the Kammas and joining another community. They repeatedly told me that even before my time, Jesus was at least one of the gods in our family. My uncle, the guru, made a comparative study of the Bible and accepted Christ as an Avatar. My mother had interest in the Gospel. But since they thought that they could not join the Church and remain Kammas they had never made a bold attempt to know the complete revelation of the Lord. This is the case with thousands of Hindus. In view of the supposed necessity of becoming a Christian by way of joining the Church, they deny themselves the privilege of knowing the Gospel at all. They avoid coming under the power of the Living Word by believing it does not belong to them.

I passed through that kind of thinking and struggle, but the power of the Gospel which I could not possibly escape encompassed me. I insisted that I must be baptized. The dean kindly informed the district missionary, Dr. E. G. Wood, and he made arrangements for my baptism in a village, Pedapalem, in a Hindu home (which has some caste converts) on Sunday, March 23, 1942. Miss Naugle went with me to that place.

When I arrived, to my great surprise, I saw my mother there. When I walked in front for baptism, my mother came and stood by my side and we were baptized together. I knew my mother and some other close relatives, including my grandmother, had for long been more or less secretly favourable to the Gospel. But for my mother to decide to be baptized along with me—this is something I cannot explain to this day. Whatever might have been her intentions then, she has made a good and effective Christian for which I am very thankful.

At the time of baptism, I certainly had a profound spiritual experience. God gave me the assurance of being forgiven and the restoration of salvation. I have experienced joy which words cannot express and which is still my very life.

> Whom having not seen, ye love; in whom, though now ye see him not, yet believing, ye rejoice with joy unspeakable and full of glory: Receiving the end of your faith, even the salvation of your souls.
>
> (I Peter 1:8, 9)

A significant change took place in my attitude toward my life work. Despite my strong determination to become a doctor, Christ simply turned me around and I joyfully and unquestioningly accepted the call to be a witness for Him preaching the Gospel to multitudes of the people who have never heard it. If I had followed my own intentions, I would have chosen the career of a doctor because that was what I wanted to be. To my great surprise, on becoming a Christian I was blessed with a firm determination to preach the Gospel. I have no explanation for this call except to quote the Scriptures from Acts 1:8:

> You cannot know times and dates which have been fixed by the Father's sole authority. But you are to be given power when the Holy Spirit has come to you. You will be witnesses to me, not only in Jerusalem, not only throughout Judea, not only in Samaria, but to the very ends of the earth. (Phillips Translation)

Along with the joy of Salvation and indeed as a part of it came the burden to share it with others, especially with non-Christians in my native Andhra.

How the Problem Looked to Dr. Pickett

In his famous book, Christian Mass Movements in India, (1933), Dr. Pickett devoted one whole chapter to "The Sudra Movement in the Telugu Country." (Andhra Pradesh) In this section, I intend to set forth the situation concerning caste converts as it then appeared to Dr. Pickett and quote heavily from him.

In Andhra Pradesh, Sudhras are numerous, influential and wealthy people. During the years 1928-1933, a great people movement took place among them. It is unfortunate that Pickett uses the term "mass movement" in the place of people movement, but I prefer the latter which Dr. McGavran defines in the following manner:

> A people movement results from the joint decision of a number of individuals whether five or five hundred ---all from the same people, which enables them to become Christians without social dislocation, while remaining in full contact with their non-Christian relatives, thus enabling other groups of that people across the years, after suitable instruction, to come to similar decisions and form Christian churches made up exclusively of members of that people.
>
> (McGavran 1970:297-298)

A people movement involves multi-individual decisions, meaning that many people participate, each making up his own mind after debating with himself and others within his group. Each individual is saved, not by going along with the crowd, but by his personal faith which led him to participate in the decision of the group.

A people movement involves mutually interdependent decisions, meaning that all who decide do so in view of what others are going to do and confident of their support in the matter.

While the homogeneous principle directs the Church's attention to the existence and significance of the many sub-groups which make up every society and warns us that the Gospel must be related to each segment of the cultural mosaic, the people movement principle relates to the process by which homogeneous units are most likely to become Christian. This process applies equally in primitive or civilized societies.

In this regard, Dr. Pickett says:

> While mass movements of Sudras to Christianity have taken place in the past, the beginning of a new movement in a Sudra caste anywhere would be highly important. But the significance of these movements is enhanced by the number of castes affected by the

> unique importance of Sudras in the Telugu Country, and by the fact that they are the first instance of mass movements of Sudras following such movements of the depressed classes in the same area. (Pickett 1933:294)

These Sudhra movements have developed in widely separated areas of at least six missions. About forty castes that belong to upper and lower middle classes were affected and within a five-year period over 15,000 became Christians in all the six missions.

> A missionary of the United Lutheran Mission, writing in June, 1932, says: 'In this district we have baptized about 1,500 Sudras in the last five years, more than half of them within the last twelve months.' (Pickett 1933:295)

The new Christians were very happy as far as their faith was concerned, but they experienced many difficulties in identifying themselves with the depressed class Christians. Pickett interviewed numbers of converts from the higher castes regarding their social relationships with the Harijan Christians, expressing his opinion in the following manner:

> The question of intermarriage is very complicated and few are willing to discuss it freely. After several inquiries had led to excited feeling and argument, we dropped the subject.
>
> In our discussion of this subject with converts from the higher castes, two considerations were almost invariably put forward by them: first that any social relation on their part with Christians of depressed classes origin would put an obstacle in the way of the conversion of their relatives and others in the higher castes, and, second, that the older Christians, converted from the Malas and the Madigas, had maintained their separate communities and opposed social relations, especially marriage across their respective caste lines, so have no right to object if the new converts from the upper castes do the same. (Pickett 1938: 65-66)

Pickett's observation regarding the feeling of caste converts about their social relationships with Harijan Christians holds good today also. Over the years, many attempts have been made to bring the two groups of Christians from the Harijans closer, but with little success. With over twenty years of experience in the Church and having opportunities to know the Christians of the Harijan community as well as caste converts, I reaffirm Dr Pickett's conclusion. It applies everywhere today.

Pickett makes a special mention of Reddys and Kammas who joined the Church in great numbers.

> The Reddys and the Kammas are the dominant castes in many villages. They own a large portion of the land and many are prosperous. Several hundred members of these castes in Guntur and Kistna Districts of British India and in adjoining areas of the Nizam's Dominions have been baptized. Thousands are friendly to Christianity. (Pickett 1938:106)

I am glad to say that the Reddys and Kammas---and Kapus too---are most responsive to the Gospel in these days. To establish this fact, I will include a case study in the next section of this treatise.

Pickett did not forget to write about Christ's work for women in Andhra. Even the members of anti-Christian movements accepted the fact that women were much benefitted by Christianity.

> A member of the often militantly anti-Christian Arya Samaj said to the writer in a village in West Godavari that the greatest value the Christian movement has brought to Andhra Desa is freedom for the minds and souls of women. He added, 'A degenerate Hinduism enslaved our women. They were condemned to illiteracy, idolatry, superstition, suffering, drudgery and dullness. The lovely things of life were all kept from them. Through Christian Missions the folly and the wrong of this treatment of our women has been convincingly demonstrated.' (Pickett 1938: 69)

In many cases in Andhra, women believed in the Lord first and then won their husbands and other relatives to the Christian faith. The following illustration by Pickett helps us to understand the remarkable influence of Christian women in India.

> Early in this study we sat one day with 400 others in a temporary structure erected at the expense of a group of propserous Hindu farmers for a series of evangelistic meetings. The most prominent Hindu of the village was in the chair. He introduced as the preacher of the afternoon an aged widow. For thirty-five minutes that preacher held the attention of her audience. Her sermon, in a language which the writer does not understand, was said to be logical, forceful and eloquent. At its close, the chairman thanked her and remarked that times were changing when a Hindu audience would listen with interest, respect and profit to an address on religion delivered by a woman.
>
> Another Hindu said to the writer after the service, 'What interested us most was her testimony. We know that she has experienced salvation. Her whole life is radiant with holiness.' (Pickett 1938: 70,71)

* * * *

Women's witness to the power of the Gospel is very important for the growth of the Church in Andhra. In the last few years, it has been my privilege to preach the Gospel to non-Christians and the response from men and women has been very satisfactory.

I conclude this section with Pickett's remark concerning the effectiveness of the converts' witness:

> Every convert is a potential evangelist and the potentialities of many converts are enormous. One Waddara was found to have near relatives in fourteen villages. Within a year of his conversion he influenced six groups in which he had relatives to enroll as catechumens. (Pickett 1938: 108)

How the Problem Looked to Me

The central problem of my life which I am describing in this thesis is the tension which arises as men and women of caste background find that becoming disciples of the Lord Jesus means that must become members of a church located in the palem and composed of Christians of the Harijan community.

This problem was before me at the time of my conversion and indeed, everyday of my life thereafter. However, my convictions concerning it were deepened during the years 1968-69 when we conducted an Ashram at Rajahmundry and to that I now turn.

Christian Ashram at Rajahmundry

Christian Ashrams play a very important part on present day India. There are about fifty Christian Ashrams in India, Ceylon, and Nepal. Ashrams have demonstrated that Christ can unite people of different creeds, castes, and colours into brotherhood.

In the words of Dr. R. Pierce Beaver, the Ashram is defined as follows: "An ashram is an ascetic community characterized by fellowship, mutual bearing of burdens, common worship, silent meditation, intercession, and study. It is living a close family life under a rule of discipline to the glory of God, to the service of the most needy, and to the communication of the Gospel. It is one form of the Indian holy life baptized into the service of Jesus Christ and His Church."

Until 1968, the Andhra Evangelical Lutheran Church had not started any Ashrams. As an experimental measure, the Board of Christian Education and Literature of our Church asked the Charlotte Swenson Memorial Bible Training School (located at Luthergiri, Rajahmundry) to conduct an Ashram programme. We gladly accepted this challenging work, conducting an Ashram during June and July of 1968. Those who attended were newly baptized women (converts), and Hindu women who were interested in knowing thc Gospel (enquirers). Our programme was conducted in an informal manner, with members being free to come and go according to their convenience. Although we began with only fifteen members, on the last day the number had grown to one hundred and five. A total of one hundred and eighty-three women and twenty-eight children came to the Ashram during this first experiment! Among those who came were Hindu enquirers belonging to different castes. They were able to live together as one family and were even able to eat together! This fellowship provided an excellent means of communicating the Gospel. The greatest joy for the converts who attended was in joining with fellow Christians at Christ Church, Luthergiri, to receive the Sacrament of the Lord's Supper.

The programme at the Ashram included Gospel messages, indigenous ways of worship like Bhajana*, and discussions which might help to answer problems. Because of the different backgrounds and family circumstances represented, many members needed personal counselling. This part of the sessions was not too effective because of crowded living conditions and the lack of enough counsellors. This is an area to be strengthened in the future.

During the academic year (July to April), the Charlotte Swenson Memorial Bible Training School conducts a Bible Training Course for girls who have had a high school or college education. Therefore, the Ashram programme could not be continued on the same scale. However, because so many of the women who attended the first session returned to the Ashram and kept bringing their relatives, an informal programme was conducted until April 20, 1969. A total of four hundred persons came to the Ashram during this time. Most of these persons were Hindus. So after closing the regular classes at the Training School, a programme for the Ashramites was announced from April 20 to 30, 1969. The response was wonderful! This time, whole families participated in the programme and a few women were baptized. When the institution closed for the summer, arrangements were made for many to participate in the Ashram programme in the future.

In December, 1968, the Ashramites invited us to give Christmas programmes in their villages among their non-

---

*Bhajana is worship accompanied by music. The congregation sits in a circle or in some other informal manner. Some members of the congregation accompany with wooden clappers, tambourines, bells, cymbals, and other small percussion instruments. Very often the song leader will sing a verse and the congregation will respond by repeating the verse or providing another verse.

Christian friends. A two-hour programme was prepared which included a Christmas drama by the students, indigenous methods of story telling, Bhajana with instruments, and a short Christmas message. Our Ashramites and Bible women were the contact persons for our entrance into the villages, giving us the invitation to come and making the necessary arrangements. It was amazing to see how much they appreciated our coming with the Christmas message, and to see how these few women are influencing whole communities. Our Ashramites paved the way to have the village leaders come, and in some villages the president of the Panchayat* presided over the function. Large crowds attended these Christmas programmes with people coming from surrounding villages. Many were relatives of the Ashramites. Some Ashramites returned to Luthergiri to share in our fellowship on Christmas day.

Many women showed extraordinary interest in the Gospel. Natural leaders, they led many others to the Ashram programme. Two I would like particularly to mention.

Addala Surayamma belongs to a middle class Hindu family. For the first time she came to the Ashram in June, 1968 and stayed only for a couple of days, then went back to her village, Madurapudi, which is ten miles away from Rajahmundry. After two weeks, she came back with her husband, Mr. Bhima Raju. Almost the first thing they asked me was whether they could buy a Bible; they read it for over three hours sitting in front of my office. From then on, Surayamma brought about 200 men and women from her village. Through her many of their relatives heard about our programme and some of them attended the Ashram.

On December 14, 1968, Surayamma and her husband invited us to have a Christmas programme at their place. They had invited many of their relatives from the surrounding villages for the function. Practically the whole village witnessed the programme and the president of their village panchayat presided over the meeting.

*Panchayat, a village council of elders, the equivalent of the New England town council, but with the informality of the old-fashioned town meeting.

We have a standing invitation to go to their village any time. Surayamma's house became a sort of meeting place for the enquirers and her husband reads the Bible for them. I certainly hope a people movement takes place there.

Another enthusiastic person is Subbayamma from Punyakshetram, about eight miles away from Rajahmundry. Just a few years ago, she and about fifteen of her relatives became Christians.

At the time of the Ashram, she brought a number of her relatives from different villages. It is amazing how much interest she took to share the Gospel with her friends and relatives. She often walked ten to fifteen miles in the hot sun to invite her friends. Many a time I remarked that she should not exert herself so much. Invariably her answer was, "The Lord gives me the strength." Her concern for her people is really remarkable.

Subbayamma's husband is still a Hindu. For some time he persecuted her; lately he changed his attitude. In 1969, they built a new house and they had a prayer meeting for the dedication instead of the customary Hindu rites. Some of us went there for the function. She is an effective witness among her people.

Though our experience with the Ashram has been little, the response of those who have participated in this programme lead us to believe that Ashrams can play an important part in this mission of the Church in Andhra Pradesh.

The Tension at the Ashram

The amazing responsiveness of the Kammas and Kapus and others from a caste background amazed me. Dozens of people indicated a desire to be baptized but hesitated because they would have had to be baptized in the Harijan Christian Church building. Almost everyday I asked myself if there was not some way for the tremendous task to be accomplished. I discussed it with some pastors and missionaries. I prayed about it. I thought about it. The problem was becoming clearer and more urgent to me. The solution I had not yet worked out. But I did later and shall describe it in chapter four.

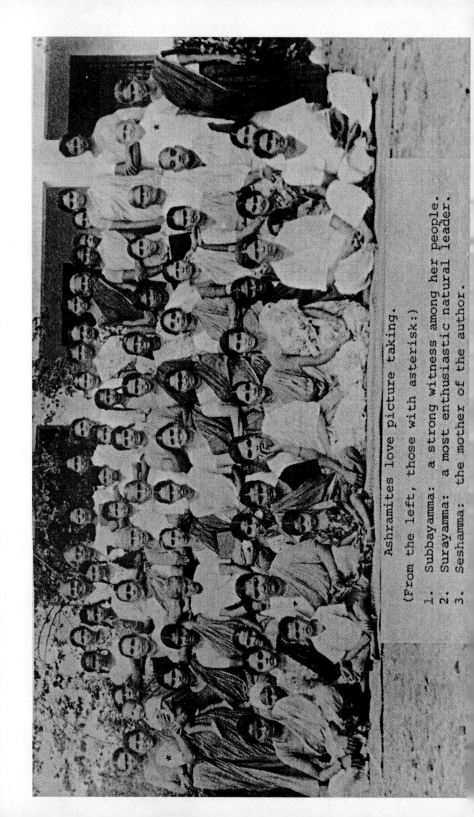

Ashramites love picture taking.

(From the left, those with asterisk:)

1. Subbayamma: a strong witness among her people.
2. Surayamma: a most enthusiastic natural leader.
3. Seshamma: the mother of the author.

Names of girls and instruments they are holding.

Seated in Front Row (L. to R.): Mary (Dakki), Suryam (Drum), Jaya Kumari (Dolak), Halleluya (Dakki)

Second Row (L. to R.): Santhosham (Chirathalu), Vasanth (Muvvalu), Krupa (Kanjari), Miss B. V. Subbamma (Kanjari), Sarani (Kanjari), Aliceamma (Thalalu), Daya (Gummatam)

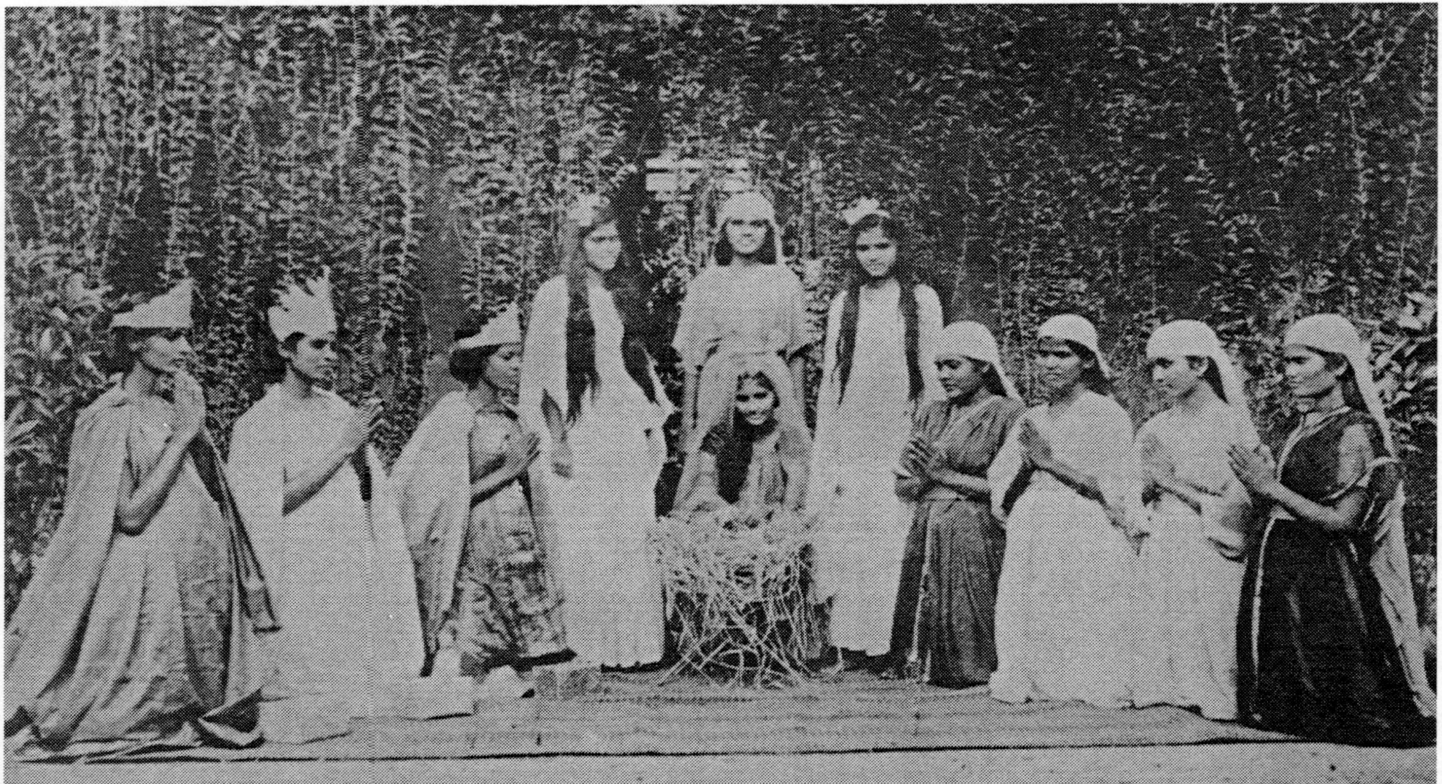

In rural villages Bible training students proclaim the Lord's birth in drama.

The story of Christ is told by means of the indigenous dance, *Burrakatha*

How the Problem Looked to the Rev. S. W. Schmitthenner

The Rev. S. W. Schmitthenner has been the president of our Andhra Evangelical Lutheran Church since January, 1969. Before that, he worked as a district evangelistic missionary for a number of years. Between 1962 and 1968, he made a survey of evangelism among Hindus and in October of that year, presented a paper to A.E.L.C. Long Range Planning Conference on the following subject, "The Structure and Outreach of the A.E.L. Church in Rural Andhra."

> As far as possible, evaluation of the existing evangelistic agencies of the Church will be based on empirical evidence gathered during the past six years of parish survey work, a survey of Bible women's work which has been made with the help of evangelistic pastors and Bible women's supervisors, studies of eight Sudhra congregations, and statistical study made of Sudhra baptisms during the past thirty years.
> (Schmitthenner 1968: 2)

I would like to present this excellent case study. I will closely follow his outline and express his ideas sometimes in my own words but mostly in his words.

Part One: The Limitations That Congregational Structure Imposes on the Outreach of the Rural Church

The Andhra Evangelical Church is based on the Harijan communities. The present Church is the result of people movements that have taken place among the Malas and Madigas from the latter part of the nineteenth century through the 1930s.

In many villages, we have separate churches for the two communities of Harijans (Malas and Madigas). In some places they both worship together, even then the congregation is not really integrated. It is a congregation with two segments.

The very location of most rural congregations hinders the outreach. Generally, the church is located in the palem which lies some distance away from the village proper.

Part Two: The Challenge — To Bring the Gospel into the Village

The Rev. S. W. Schmitthenner has stated:

> If the church is to make a real impact upon society in Andhra, the Gospel must be brought to the Sudhras and higher caste Hindus who make up more than 75 per cent of the population. The Reddys, Kammas, Telegas, and Kapus are the dominant castes of the State.
> (Schmitthenner 1968:7)

He believes that the widespread influence of the Reddys, Kammas, and Kapus throughout the other castes of the village as well as their capacity to absorb and introduce new ideas has great implications for those who seek to permeate all of society with the Gospel of Christ. He added:

> Never before have the caste people showed such an interest in the Gospel. Bible women supervisors and evangelistic pastors agree that the doors are open much wider than they were even five years ago.
> (Schmitthenner 1968:8)

Surely the Church faces a great opportunity to evangelize the Sudhras who are so ready for the Gospel. Now the question is, how can the Church best meet the needs of this section of society?

Part Three: Congregations not Meeting the Challenge

Even good congregations have failed to bring the Gospel to Sudhras. The author gave the example of Yendagendi, as a model congregation. Of that congregation, 76 per cent of the adults are active, communing members and they give generously for the Church. In every way, they are exemplary Christians.

Even that kind of congregation however, Pastor Schmitthenner stated, fails to witness to the caste people in the village. If an exemplary village church fails, one can imagine the degree of witness other churches are giving or not giving.

A social reason for this failure, the segmented nature of society in an Indian village, makes it difficult for even a successful method or idea to spread from the palem to the Sudhra part of the village. The writer remarked:

> For the most part, the Hindu looks upon the Christian palem as a Harijan palem (Paul Wiebe, Ph.D. thesis) The idea of Christ appeals to him, but not the idea of patterning his style of life and worship after that of the Harijans, (Schmitthenner 1968: 10)

Among attitudes of Christians that are detrimental to the spread of the Gospel, the most critical failure on the part of the congregation is lack of evangelical motivation. Most Christians are not concerned with the need of Hindus for the Gospel. They do not really feel that discipling Hindus is part of their Christian responsibility though they do talk about it a great deal. Also, the attitude of the pastors in three of the five Lutheran Synods were graded, with the help of the concerned synod evangelistic pastors and other consultants, into three categories: First, those who are concerned about Sudhras and make special efforts to reach them; second, those who while they give minimum pastoral services to Sudhras, seldom if ever visit Sudhra Christians in their homes; and third, those who by their attitude and neglect actually obstruct the work of the Gospel among the Sudhras.

As shown in the following table, out of some 103 pastors, 35 studied fall in the first category, 48 in the second, and 20 in the third:

Total number surveyed	Positive concern	Minimum concern	Negative concern
103	35	48	20

He makes the following conclusion.

> While it is gratifying to note that one-third of the pastors evaluated have a positive interest in Sudhra work and are taking some initiative for this in their parishes, it is very sad to find that more than half of the pastors will not go out of their way to work among Sudhras, and do not feel the urgency or importance of this work.
> (Schmitthenner 1968: 11)

Part Four: Special Ministry to the Sudhras

For the past twenty-five years or more, the work among the Sudhras has been carried on largely by people especially called and appointed for this work---the evangelistic pastors, the evangelists, and the Bible women. This special ministry has been directed by the Board of Evangelism of our Church. The following table shows the gain in number of Sudhras and other non-Harijan baptisms during the past five years:

Caste Baptism Gains: 1962-1967

SYNOD	caste converts	baptisms 1963-67	joined sects	died or left
E. Godavari	807	581	91	50
W. Godavari	675	358	37	94 left 121 died
E. Guntur	725	289	139	
C. Guntur	918	241	154	60
W. Guntur	1493	331		79 left 105 died

SYNOD	total losses	net total converts	percent of gain
E. Godavari	141	1247	54
W. Godavari	242	791	17
E. Guntur	139	875	20
C. Guntur	214	945	3
W. Guntur	202	1622	8
		total 5480	

Caste converts make up only 2% of Andhra Evangelical Lutheran Church members (Survey, S.W. Schmittenner)

Part Five: Special Ministry to Sudhras---Women's Work

Apart from the Palnad, the main outreach of the Church has been to women.

Percentage of Men, Women and Children: Sudhra Christians

	Men	%.	Women	%	Children	%
E. Godavari	258	20	847	68	142	12
W. Godavari	71	9	671	86	49	5
C. Guntur	247	26	502	52	196	22
W. Guntur	567	35	578	36	477	29

It is obvious from the above that there is much more work being done among women; women are the ones coming into the Church. Some have argued that this pattern is unfortunate, because unless whole families are brought into the Church there will not be sustained growth. They feel that since women have a subordinate place in society the evangelistic effort of the Church will not lead to a real entrance into Hindu society.

Sociological study, however, indicates that religious change can best be brought about in Andhra through women, In South India society the mother-son relationship is the most crucial of all family relationships. (Francis L. K. Shu, Psychological Anthropology, Kinship and Ways of Life) The influence of the mother over her sons, daughter-in-law, and grandchildren is very great, especially in a joint family. The grandmother is the one most concerned in giving religious and moral training, teaching tradition, and legends. (Indian Women, Margaret Cormiok)

Outreach of Convert Women. From the study of the eight Sudhra congregations, it is evident that many convert women spread the Gospel among their own relatives. To give a few examples, Chittamma of Veeravasaram has brought her sister and brother-in-law and sixteen other sisters, cousins, daughters-in-law and nieces to the Lord. I know this lady personally. One time she took two weeks voluntary training course in our Bible School and I also visited her place. In a most informal and natural way, she passes on the Gospel.

At Rayalam, B. Venkayamma has been instrumental in bringing eight others to Christ. There are dozens of converts like these who bring neighbours, friends, and members of their kinship group into the Church as full members.

The Bible Women's Work is vital to the mission of the Church. Two hundred and fifteen Bible women in the Church comprise the main force of evangelistic workers. All doors are open to the women, but not to men workers. The strength of the Bible woman lies in the personal friendships she forms with Hindu women. She teaches according to a syllabus that has been carefully prepared based on the central message of the Scriptures. Her work has been greatly blessed.

Evangelistic Parishes. In his thoughtful 1968 report, the Rev. S. W. Schmitthenner proposed parishes for Sudhras. These would be made up of prayer groups which are already established, with an evangelistic pastor whose full-time responsibility is to shepherd these small congregations and to bring in new members. To form each Sudhra parish, there is need to go across existing (Harijan) parish boundaries. The Rev. S. W. Schmitthenner says in his fine description of the Sudhra Parish Plan (Long Range Planning Conference of October 1968 at Bhimavaram: Appendix 6)

> The traditions of the Church that must be set aside if we are really to make the most of the open door are these:
>
> a) Strict adherence to geographical boundaries of parishes. It is time we realize that social boundaries are equally important. For a pastor working in 15 palems to claim that no one else should work in his villages is absurd, if he is not working in any of the villages proper.
>
> b) Ideal that all believers should worship together in one place in each village. After 125 years we must realize that we are not practising this in most places. We cannot expect from the Sudhras this ideal which the Malas and Madigas have not been able to attain in so many generations.

The conviction to which God has brought me is one to which he has brought and is bringing many others of His servants in Andhra Pradesh. I am confident that it is shared and will be shared by many pastors and bishops and lay men and women as they meditate on the biblical way to enter the door which God opens before us during the seventies. Since social boundaries are more important than geographical, a diagram will make this clearer.

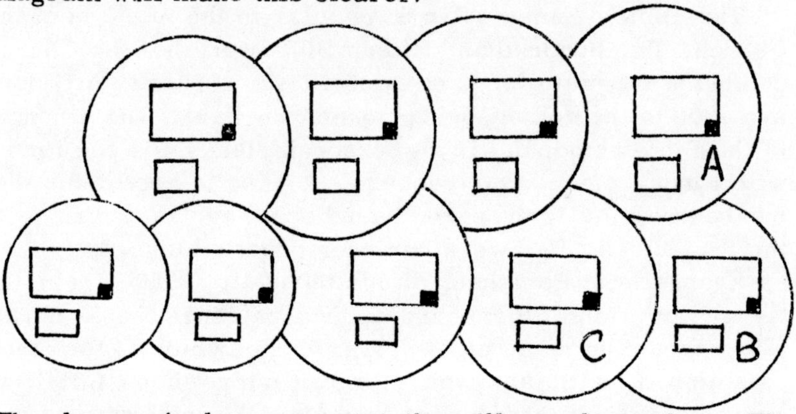

The large circles represent the village plus palem. The small squares represent the existing churches (Harijan Christians plus converts). The large squares represent the caste sections of the village. Within them, the little solid squares are the existing prayer groups. Pastor Schmitthenner's proposal means that several villages constitute one evangelistic parish in one Sudhra parish. For example, above A, B, and C might be considered as one Sudhra parish and one worker be assigned to it.

Pastors called to this work will be evangelistic pastors, selected by the Board of Evangelism and Missions. Their task would be to win families of Sudhras to Christ and add them to these 'solid' churches. They should be the kind of men who will give themselves completely to ministry among the Sudhras. When available, experienced Sudhra pastors should be called to this work.

The advantages of this plan are many. By strengthening these nucleus congregations with frequent visits and regular teaching, we can help them to become a great force of outreach. The prayer groups planted by Bible women will be nurtured, the men also will be reached.

I am glad to report that following Pastor Schmithenner's proposal in June, 1969, the Church established three special

Sudhra parishes as an experimental measure. In these parishes, "Sudhra parish" pastors do the shepherding of the converts and communicate the Gospel to the caste people. In this kind of evangelistic effort, the converts will be great promoters along with the pastor and Bible women. The formal action of the Church—quoted on the next page—gives the aims of this new programme and the pattern of the special parishes.

Special Committee on Evangelism Parishes
Implementation Plan: (Ref. LCM 148/473)
Implemented from June 1, 1969
Rev. S. W. Schmitthenner, Chairman.

Voted that the following plan be adopted in implementing the Evangelistic parishes in the Synods:

I. Aims of this new Programme:
1. To provide weekly or more frequent visitation and prayer service for all converts and inquirers.
2. To provide for converts to partake of the Lord's supper once a month.
3. To provide them the experience of being a real part of the congregation.
4. To evangelize the men in the convert families.
5. To encourage congregational growth through family relationships and among neighbours of the converts.
6. To provide the witness of worship in the midst of the Hindu locality.
7. To provide experience in Christian fellowship between Christians of different caste backgrounds through Maha Sabhas and through the Ashram programme.
8. To teach stewardship from the start of congregational life.
9. To bring these parishes to support their pastors within 5 years.
10. To search out young men and women from caste Christian families for training in evangelism and in the ministry.

II. Formation of Parishes—West Godavari District:

A. West Godavari Synod	1st Parish
1. Gollavanithippa	2. Rayalam
3. Seesalee	4. Veeravasaram
5. Perugupalem	6. Pennada-Vissakoderu

The pastor should reside at Bhimavaram in the evangelistic pastor's house. The pastor will be paymaster for the Bible Women in the above villages, but those Bible Women will work under the charge of the person-in-charge of Bible Women's work.

(Pastor for this parish—Rev. M. Joseph)

B. West Godavari Synod	2nd Parish
1. Attili	2. Moyyeru
3. Akudicipadu	4. Varadalapalem
5. Kesavaramraju	

The pastor should reside at Attili in rented house. He will be pastor for the Bible Women in the above villages who will work under the person-in-charge of Bible Women's work.

(Pastor for this parish—Rev. Alamuri Samuel Babu Rao)

III. Budget of Parishes, West Godavari:

	Parish I	Parish II
Pastor's salary	208	200
Incidentals	40	40
Rent		25
	248	265
June-Dec. 7 months	1,736	1,885
Expected offerings	136	200
	1,600	1,655

Total 2,840 Additional needed 415

Budget already sanctioned for 1969 June-Dec. 2,840

There is a great urgency to start new patterns of evangelism among Hindus (caste people). The doors are opened for communicating the Gospel. Though Christians are a minority, our Indian constitution gives great freedom to proclaim the Good News.

> Some of the main provisions of the constitution, in the chapter on fundamental rights, guaranteed, subject to public order, morality, and health to all citizens, freedom of conscience and the right freely to profess, practise and propagate religion; untouchability, the age old scourge of India, was abolished and its practice in any form forbidden. (Veda prakash Luthera 1964:2)

Another important factor is this, that before India became independent in 1947, Christianity was identified with the foreigners because of British rule, or with the outcasts. After freedom, the Church can no longer be identified with the foreigners. It must no longer be strictly limited to the Harijan community.

There is no way of knowing how long the present openness will continue, so the churches must be planted in these responsive homogeneous groups before the doors close. When the Church realizes her responsibility to evangelize caste people and provide them an opportunity to become Christians within their own homogeneous units, there will be tremendous growth of the Andhra Evangelical Lutheran Church.

4

The Crucial Problem in Discipling Hindus

Can They Become Christians in Their Own Culture?

The Cross of Jesus Christ, which is the centre of the history of the world as of the life of the Church, constitutes a call to all men without exception to be converted to God in order that they may know Him and willingly play their part in the fulfillment of His purpose for the universe. The Church must help men hear this call. She must not put unbiblical barriers before them to make their turning more difficult or impossible. At the same time, she must put clearly before them the biblical conditions for becoming Christians. These barriers the Church is not authorized to remove.

> The offense of the cross is one basic barrier to becoming Christian. To accept the truth that one is a sinner whose salvation depends not at all on what he does but entirely on his accepting what Jesus Christ has done for him on the cross, affronts his ego. To repent of one's sins and turn from them is another basic barrier to discipleship. Openly to confess Christ before men, be baptized in His name, and join the Church is a third obstacle. To those who accept the authority of the Scriptures, these barriers must remain. But the Church and her emissaries are constantly tempted to add others. (McGavran 1970: 4)

These other barriers are not recognized by the Bible. Hence, they should not be imposed. For example, from the beginning of the Christian Church, it is evident that men like to become Christians without crossing racial, linguistic, caste, and class barriers. If then, to become Christian the Church requires men to worship in other than their own mother tongue, or marriage outside their normal marriage market, "break caste," or renounce their own culture, she is imposing a man-made and unnecessary barrier. To become a Christian must be a religious decision rather than racial. It must be seen as a move to make Jesus Christ supreme in one's life—and not as merely a move from one social group or race to another. Whenever it is presented as a racial move ("Come join our caste, leave your caste"), the growth of the Church is exceedingly low. In presenting the Gospel to the world, the main problem the Church has to deal with is how to present Christ so that men can truly follow Him without leaving their kindred. The following statement on conversion from the "Findings of the National Consultation on the Mission of the Church in Contemporary India held at Nasrapur," March 1966, gives special light:

> (c) The conversion of a man or a group to Christ is the work of the Holy Spirit. It is a new creation and not merely an extension of the boundaries of the existing Church. The new converts should, therefore, be recognisable (sic) as the first fruit for Christ of the society to which they belong, bringing their specific gifts into the fellowship. This means that the Church must not seek to impose its whole traditional style of life upon the new convert. We have to confess that because this has often been done in the past, baptism has been made to appear as an act by which a person repudiates his ancient cultural heritage and accepts an alien culture. So long as this is so we cannot judge those who while confessing faith in Jesus, are unwilling to be baptised (sic). As we have said in another paper we regard it as urgent that the Church should take much more seriously the whole culture of India, which must provide the forms in which India's offering of herself to Christ is to be made. With the emer-

gence of an urban, secular culture the identification of baptism with a cultural transition is being progressively weakened and we rejoice in this fact. In the perspective of the Bible conversion is "turning from idols to serve a living and true God" and not moving from one culture to another, or from one community to another community as it is understood in the communal sense in India today.

(d) Nevertheless there are certain given elements which belong to the proper character of the Church at all places and at all times. These include---the Scriptures, the Sacraments of Baptism and Lord's Supper, the ministry, and a corporate life where members are committed to an active fellowship, prayer, witness and service. As we understand God's revelation in Jesus, we are required to offer to all men all these things which belong to full discipleship. But we acknowledge that there are many who have turned to the Lord in genuine love and obedience and who have not accepted all these elements of discipleship as we understand them. We rejoice in every such evidence of the work of Christ and seek the fellowship of such persons while continuing to testify to the meaning of full discipleship as we believe our Lord intends it.

(e) Since conversion is the work of the Holy Spirit the Church must be sensitive to discern where the Holy Spirit is working to draw men to Christ and must be willing to follow where He leads. (Report 1966: 12-13)

It is always easy to slip into legalism and to obscure the Gospel. When we approach an unbeliever, what is our message? That he should break caste, leave his social structure and thus "join a church"? Or is our message that he accept Christ as Saviour and Lord, and within his own social group and among those whom he can influence personally, multiply cells of Christian fellowship that meet the needs of daily spiritual life?

Let us look into the biblical data to find the proper answer for the above question. God desires to meet every man and interact with him in his culture and in terms of that culture. According to the Old Testament, God revealed Himself to the

Hebrew people in terms of the Hebrew language and culture. But if we examine the New Testament, the same God revealed Himself to the Greco-Roman world in terms of first-century Greco-Roman languages and culture. The illustration of Peter and Cornelius makes the matter clear. In Acts 10:15, God's revelation came to Peter in terms of Hebrew culture and he responded in the same cultural context. As we read in Acts 10, God made Peter responsible to carry the revelation to Cornelius, a Roman, a member of the Latin culture. "Peter could easily assume that only Hebrew culture was a suitable vehicle of God's communication and only a Hebrew type of response acceptable to God. To Peter, Roman culture and Roman people were alike unacceptable to God." (Kraft 1963:180) But in a vision, God asked Peter to kill and eat animals which Peter profoundly believed were unclean and thus made him to understand that at least one Roman person was acceptable to God. In Acts 10:13 (Phillip's translation), Peter makes the following statement. "I can now see that God is no respector of persons, but that in every nation the man who reverences him and does what is right is acceptable to him."

> The record goes on to indicate that a considerable number of Cornelius' relations and intimate friends responded to the message delivered by Peter and received from God the confirmation that they had been accepted by Him, without the necessity of their first becoming Jews. (Kraft 1963: 180-181)

The Holy Spirit led the Apostolic Church to understand that the Gentiles need not be required to become Jews to become Christians. Dr. Kraft, discussing the present situation in missionary work, makes the following observation:

> Much of modern effort is, in effect, promoting an approach to Christianity more akin to that of the first-century Judaizers than to that of Paul and Peter. It has merely substituted Western culture for Hebrew culture as the sine qua non for God's acceptance of man. (Kraft 1963: 183)

In India, as in many other Asian countries, the Church to a very large extent, took over the foreign patterns of institution, liturgy and theology, incorporating only a very small degree of indigenous cultural values. The foreignness of the Church in India is a serious stumbling block to many.

> The failure on the part of both missionaries and Indian Christians to naturalize Christianity in the country, their failure to learn anything from Hindu philosophy and to evolve an Indian Christian theology in which both the strands of the Indian Christian heritage are woven into a new pattern acceptable to the Indian mind. (Paul D. Rajahiah 1952: 106)

As I have already said, Charles H. Kraft expresses his strong opinion in this matter.

> Missions have had and continue to have a major hand in the process of Westernization. They have in most cases exported Western culture at its best and have acted worthily as ambassadors of the culture (including its religious aspect) within which they have developed. (Kraft 1963: 186)

If the Church in India today is truly to be the first fruit for Christ, it should devote more thought and energy to finding worthier forms in which its worship and witness may be expressed. The foreigness of the Indian Church is a stumbling block to many men of other faiths, and also a great hindrance to the growth of the Indian Church. This situation calls for an indigenization of the present Church in Andhra and in the whole of India.

But what is indigenization? There are many ethnic groups and cultures in India. The Church may become indigenous in one of these and yet be quite foreign to the others. My immediate concern is how to start churches in Andhra which are indigenous to the Hindus. So I confine myself to this aspect.

First of all, let us come to a clear understanding of the term "indigenous." In much of the missions' thinking, a Church which is "self-governing, self-supporting, and self-propagating" is an "indigenous church." I agree with William A. Smalley that this is a false diagnosis.

In this connection, he says:

> An indigenous church is a group of believers who live out their life, including their socialized Christian activity, in the patterns of the local society, and

> for whom any transformation of that society comes out of their felt needs under the guidance of the Holy Spirit and the Scriptures. (Smalley, 1967, 150)

As I have already explained in Chapter I, the social structure in Andhra Pradesh demands the recognition of the differences in culture among different homogeneous groups like Harijans and other caste groups. "By homogeneous society we mean one in which most of or all the people participate in the common life in more or less the same way." (Nida 1960:96) For many valid reasons, the caste people and the Harijans are to be considered as two different cultures, even though living in the same areas.

> Class differences in any society are based, not on a single criterion but on a number of factors which usually combine such qualities and possessions as money, heritage, education, leadership ability, and special talents, for example in acting, music, art, and oratory. (Nida 1960: 98)

From ages past, Harijans were the underprivileged class, did not own lands and mostly served the rest of the society. Because of the missions' work and also of the government support, the economic standard of Harijans as well as the Harijan Christians has been much improved. But still the difference in income between this community and the caste community is very great. In housing, the caste people live in a much better locality, most of them have comfortable homes and some of them live in big houses with all the modern conveniences. In Harijan localities, houses are very small and most are thatched, with mudwalls. Since the land is in the hands of the caste people, they eat better food, and are much better nourished.

For all practical purposes, these two classes must be treated as the different homogeneous units. Both naturally want to become Christians in their own cultures.

Indeed, looked at in one way, this is what has been happening. During the years 1927-1933, about 25,000 Sudhras became Christians. J. W. Pickett, in his famous 1933 Volume, devoted an entire chapter to the Sudhra movements to Christ. (1933: 294). Significantly he pointed out that very few Sudhras became Christians when they had to cross the caste lines, but many came to Christian faith, seeing the possibility of remaining socially within their own community. Dr. McGavran in Understanding Church Growth similarly says:

> Some thinkers on missions have assumed that this principle (that men like to become Christians without crossing racial and class barriers) holds only among primitives and "untouchables"; but there is no reason to believe that their assumption is true. The principle was true with the Jews who were among the most able races of the Roman World. It was true with the European tribes who were far from primitive. It was true among the Sudhras of Andhra Pradesh. It was true among the Moslems in Indonesia. Is it not a very human trait? Can we not assume that the great turnings which will take place in the years to come will be among men who become Christians without renouncing their culture and kindred.

We can see how true this is in the establishment and growth of the Malabar Syrian Christian Church. According to tradition, St. Thomas came to India and his first converts were high caste people. This Church naturally grew among its own high caste people. The orthodox Syrian Church today is composed almost exclusively of high caste people. In short, the Church grew only among one homogeneous group. People like to become Christians without crossing ethnic barriers. As we have seen in Chapter III, there is much evidence that caste people in Andhra today are responsive to the Gospel. They need freedom to become Christians within their own community.

As church growth theory states, the population of each modern nation is a great mosaic of sub-cultures and societies, and every individual has stamped upon him his own people's customs and its ways of thinking. Men are more likely to accept innovation when they can do it without crossing racial, linguistic, or social barriers. Individuals are also more likely to become Christians under these conditions. Christians can persuade their fellow men to follow Christ into a church "of our people"; but when they urge others to become disciples of Christ in a church which is obviously not of "our people," they have little power to persuade.

Bruno Gutmann, a Lutheran theologian and missionary to Africa, wrote with conviction that man must be treated not as an individual but as a member of an organic social unit. Quoting him, Beyerhaus writes the following:

> Uprooted from the community, an individual convert is deprived of social relations essential to his full self-realization. Therefore, Gutmann argues, for the sake of the Church, missionaries must not remain inactive while the traditional social institutions disintegrate. Still less should the missionary seek to destroy these institutions. Rather should he seek to relate them to the life of the growing Church. Gutmann fully realizes that the powerful ties of the clan (caste) often make it difficult for the individual to join the Church, but he urges that this difficulty should be borne, in the hope that ultimately not just an isolated individual or even a single family, but the whole clan or tribe may be converted. Only on such a basis, he believes, can the indigenous Church be built. (Beyerhaus and Lefever 1968: 51)

Gutmann certainly gives hearty support to the church growth theory which stresses heavily the great commission to "Go therefore and make disciples of Ta Ethne. . . ." We read also in Luke 24:47, "Repentance and forgiveness of sin should be preached in His name to Ta Ethne." The term literally means the "kindreds," the "ethnic groups" of the world. This is the basis for the "homogeneous unit principle" which says that the Church should direct its message to the peoples of the world, rather than to "people" in general.

The eminent Bishop Newbigin of the Church of South India puts his finger on this question of culture change from one homogeneous group to another and in The Finality of Christ says that the Gentile converts were not asked to become Jewish Christians, but they were baptized and attained the status of Christians equal to that of the circumcised Jewish Christians. (1969: 102-104)

In South India in the seventeeth century, one famous missionary---Robert di Nobili---identified himself with the Hindus and practised indigenous methods of evangelizing high caste Brahmins and had great response from them. He was---and is---terribly criticized. Theologians and church leaders misunderstood him. It is most interesting that Bishop Newbigin makes a reference (1969:105) to his work in the following manner:

> Robert di Nobili's Brahman converts in Madurai (town in South India) were not incorporated into Portuguese mission stations, but they were baptized and received Holy Communion. If di Nobili's critics had not been successful in discrediting him it could have happened that these converts would have profoundly changed the character of the Indian Christian community as we know it today. One could wish that it had been so.

Should They Necessarily Become the Members of the Existing Church

As we know the majority of Christians in Andhra today are of Harijan background. From ages past, they have lived in separate localities, hence, since becoming Christians they have naturally built their churches in their own residential areas. Moreover,

> The Indian Christians have always stood aloof from the rest of the citizens of Andhra as a distinct community and have segregated themselves socially and intellectually---or perhaps have been pushed out by the other communities. The Indian Christian has always been regarded, with considerable justification, as a "stranger in his own land and alien to his own culture." (Paul Rajaiah 1952: 108)

Of course, the main issue is that the Harijans and the caste Hindus are in two different homogeneous units as we have explained in the first part of this chapter. Church growth theory affirms that to attempt to plant one large conglomerate Church composed of a few Christians from each and every subculture, arguing that brotherhood demands it and insisting on integration first whether the Church grows or not, is both a self-defeating policy and not required by Biblical faith.

It is true that we are all "one in Christ." As Paul told the Ephesians (2:14):

> For He is our peace, who has made us both one, and has broken down, the dividing wall of hostility, by abolishing in His flesh the law of commandments and ordinances, that He might create in Himself one new man in place of two . . .

It is to be noted, however, that He creates "One new man in place of two" in Himself. Jews and Gentiles---or other classes and races who scorn and hate one another---must be discipled before they can really be made one.

It is most important to realize that Paul's admonitions for brotherhood were addressed to people already Christians. Whereas the real problem facing the churches in Andhra is how to bring Hindus to Christ. Many want to come; but they also want to worship Him in their own localities. The spread of the church into Hindu localities will eventually work for brotherhood. Church growth theory says that the greatest step toward brotherhood is to bring the segments (the homogeneous units) of society to repentance and faith in Jesus Christ.

First, let us consider how non-Christian populations accept Christ.

> The risen Lord made no mistake when He commanded His disciples to begin in Jerusalem and proceed to Judea. In both places, the Holy Spirit led the Christians to witness exclusively to Jews. Only after the one-people Church grew strong among the Jews, did He lead them out to win the Gentiles. When the Christian religion is beginning, in certain pieces of the mosaic of mankind (often only in one piece of it) Christian mission should base its policies on the principle that men like to become Christian without leaving their own folk, when Christian cells are starting to spread through a tribe, clan, class (caste) or segment of society, missions should work and pray to disciple that unit out to its fringes. (McGavran 1970:21)

The dedicated Christian in discipled populations is critical of allowing one kind of people to form congregations of its own.

But to have church growth among different cultures and homogeneous units, it is essential to have separate congregations and churches growing naturally in each ethnic unit in the population.

Before we conclude whether it is right or wrong to have separate congregations for caste converts, it is important to know the true meaning of the Church and its mission.

The Church is a company of people called out by God for a specific Mission. "Mission comes from a Latin word 'misso' meaning 'to send,' and therefore, to speak of the Church's 'Mission' is to say that the Church is sent by God, for a special purpose." (Wright n.d.: 5) God calls people with a special purpose of sending them on a mission. "It is not enough to say that the Church HAS a mission. The Church IS a mission." (Wright n.d.: 15) D. T. Niles in his book, Upon the Earth, described very well the Church's mission. He said,

> First of all, the Church's mission is to be the people of God. Redeemed by Christ and raised from death in Him by the Holy Spirit, the Christian community exists as the result and the demonstration of the facts of the Gospel. "You are the light of the world," Jesus said (Matthew 5:14). The Christian community cannot escape this responsibility. (Niles 1962: 73)

"Secondly, the Church's mission is to be the people of God everywhere in every situation, in every land and nation, in all areas of life." (Niles 1962:75) Christ was sent into the world and He is the outstanding missionary to mankind. The Church's mission is the continuance of the mission of its Lord. Therefore, the Church's mission is Christ's mission. It is directed to the whole world. The elect people are the Church, but they are elect, as Christ was, not to privilege but to service. If they forget this and try to monopolize God's call and gift, they fall into the error of the old Israel and cease to be the true Israel of God.

Dr. Douglas Webster in his book, Yes to Mission , summarized the mission of the Church under the following seven headings. Affirmation, Proclamation, Subordination, Penetration, Mediation, Integration, and Consummation. The Church is an affirming community in that it ought to make certain clear affirmations such as God is love, Jesus is the Lord, Christ died for our sins.

Secondly, the Church which affirms must also proclaim. Thirdly, by subordination he means that ministers of the Church are servants for Jesus sake. He supports this with statements made by Paul in II Corinthians 4:5 and I Corinthians 4:1. Here Paul speaks of missionaries as "Christ's" underlings. By two metaphors of light and salt, Dr. Webster explains the responsibility of the Church to penetrate into the world. This penetration of the Church must still keep the Church distinct from the world. When he speaks of the Church as mediation, he tries to explain that the Gospel of this salvation brought by Jesus is to be mediated to men through the ministry of men and women consecrated for the mission of the Church.

By integration, he emphasizes the fact that once the believers of Christ begin to experience unity with him, that experience must find its expression in its full measure in the total structure of the Church in its universality or catholicity, Galations 3:26-29.

Lastly, for Dr. Webster, consummation is to be understood in terms of the mission which began with God and ends with God, like creation.

From our reading of Scripture, we are led to affirm that the Church is people, in God's purpose it is His people set in many places, yet one in every place (Romans 12:4-5; I Corinthians 12:14-27; Ephesians 4:4-16). All those who are incorporated into the Body of Christ are called by baptism to share in His mission: to be light, salt, leaven in the world (Romans 6:1-11 cf. 12:1-2; Matthew 5:13-16 cf, 13:33). Knowing the present state of the Church in Andhra Pradesh as well as in the world, we have to acknowledge that the Church is far from being in actuality what God intends.

> The Church and all its organizations and institutions and agencies and commissions and boards and programs and printed materials and audio-visuals and consultations and conventions and social statements and motions and minutes have no valid significance except as they contribute to God's mission to man. The two important elements in the situation are

God and man. (Mangum 1968: 3)

There must be a drastic renewal of the Church in its structure and also its inner life.

> In Andhra, we have to recognize that the existing churches have developed into "waiting churches" of largely Harijan background into which Hindus are expected to come. The inherited structures of the existing churches stress and embody this static outlook. One may say that the churches in Andhra are in grave danger of perpetuating "come structures" instead of replacing them by "go structures." They expect the Hindus to "come" to where they are. One may say that inertia has replaced the dynamism of the Gospel and of participation in the mission of God. (World Council of Churches 1968: 19)

Alas! Our own structures operate as obstacles and hindrances preventing the proclamation of the Gospel reaching the receptive people of our state.

Change will not be easy. I am aware of the fact that the general feeling of Christendom is not to disturb the present form or function of the Church. Of course, the belief that the Church is a divinely constituted institution conditions the thinking of the members. But structure is never sacred. If we go back in the history of missions, however, we will discover that the Churches far from building according to one pattern, tended to take on, either consciously or unconsciously, the organizational form of the state system under which they were founded. In general scholars agree that through two thousand years churches have demonstrated great variety in their organization and procedures. It is consequently entirely in line with the historical practice of the Church that we should fit the churches to the needs of the populations becoming Christian.

Benz points out that

> Before Constantine, the major Christian communities in the East and West had their individual creeds, their individual systems of doctrine, their treasure of special traditions in all realms of life. The genius of the early Christians has decided that the Church, to achieve the widest possible influence, must model

itself upon the organization of the secular station. (Durnbaugh 1968: 27)

David O. Moberg represents Church as a social institution and says that "The Church" is synonymous with "organized religion." "From its earliest origins in pre-historic antiquity, organized religion has been a dynamic institution continually in flux." (Durnbaugh 1968: 514) He compares the Church to a motion picture and a soundtrack which record changes as they occur.

Let us turn to Martin Luther and examine how he dealt with the matter of church organization. He was faced with the practical problems of organizing an evangelical Church in Germany.

In 1526, he published his own vernacular mass since he saw the need for it in the common tongue for the "simple unlearned layfolk." This was a shock for many and they stood around and gaped, hoping to see something new, just as if they were holding a service among the Turks or the heathen in a public square or out in a field. What he thought really needful was a "truly evangelical order." This he thought should be held privately for those "who want to be Christians in earnest and who profess the Gospel with hand and mouth." The following was his suggestion as to how such a group should be formed. "(They) should sign their names and meet alone in a house somewhere to pray, to read, to baptize, to receive the sacrament, and do other Christian works." (Durnbaugh 1968: 3)

If the Church is really the people of God, sent by Him, into all the strata of society, and into all the busy life of His world, if the laity are really the front line of the Church's mission, if the local church really exists in order to be God's ministry to the situation where He has put it, then we must reshape the structures.

In the words of the New Delhi Assembly of the World Council of Churches,

> If this penetration of the world by the lay witness is an essential part of God's plan for His Church, we must examine the conventional structures of our churches to see whether they assist or hinder the work of evangelism. We must ask whether we do not

> too easily fall into the habit of thinking of the Church as the Sunday congregation, rather than as the laity scattered abroad in every department of daily life.

This points out the fact that the old structures are no longer relevant---indeed, that they often hinder the Church from doing its real job. We must follow the good example of Italian designers.

> The story behind Olivetti and Necchi is significant. In each case, the canny manufacturer took his design problem to an artist, with this commission: "Restudy the whole problem of this machine, then determine how it ought to look in a modern world, ignoring all previous concepts. (Michener 1969: 158)

Now we refer to three new forms of congregational life: The Church of Ministers. All seventy members of the "Church of the Saviour" in Washington are called "ministers." They run a coffee house in a good area of the capital. People come there and sit for awhile. They serve coffee there and "gossip the Gospel" freely with the people. (Kenyon E. Wright, n.d., 3 & 4)

The second type is The Church of the Holy Carpenter, Hong Kong. For six days, this place will be kept busy working with machines. On the seventh day, a curtain is drawn aside at the top to reveal the altar with a picture of Christ working in the carpenter's shop---and there, in the midst of their tools and machines, that congregation worships God in sincerity and truth.

The third one is A Congregation of House Churches. In Port Glasgow, Scotland, we find one of a number of examples of a pattern in which the weekly service in the church building itself is only a small part of the church's life, which is mainly expressed by house churches all over the parish area. These house groups in their worship and prayers are concerned with the immediate area (a street or two) in which they work. They try to carry out real positive service to the people of their small area who are in any kind of need or difficulty. Another similar church in America has no church building at all. They do not intend to build a church because they feel that would destroy the mobility and missionary character of their church.

I have mentioned these various forms of churches to emphasize the fact that churches in Andhra facing the great opportunities of discipling Hindus must not fear new forms. The Church all over the world as it is renewed uses new forms. Why should not we?

Should They Necessarily Become the Members of Another Homogenous Unit?

Evaluation of the Present Set-Up

Are we evangelizing them in the New Testament pattern? Under the history of Protestant Churches in Andhra Pradesh, I made special mention of the evangelistic programme of different Churches. It is a fact that all the Churches are trying to include evangelism in their programmes. But evangelism means different things to different people and Churches. On the whole, many Christians in Andhra are committed to a seed sowing evangelism. They have a theology of this which might also be called a theology of search.

> It maintains that in Christian mission the essential thing is not the finding, but going everywhere and preaching the Gospel---for which there is some excellent Biblical authority. (McGavran 1970: 34)

Dr. McGavran describes four factors under which search theology framed its major beliefs. In the first instance, it arose in the face of indifference at home and hostility abroad. It was believed that search only was God's will. Secondly, a vast relativism, based on the study of non-Christian religions, has buttressed search theology.

The third chief factor arose because of the big gap between the standard of living in the West and that of the masses in Africa and Asia. The missionary and the boards saw great need everywhere for food, education, and health and kept busy with institutional and other social uplift work. Thus, instead of discipling the nations, the missionary was pushed into all kinds of philanthropic work. "These were defended as 'a preparation for the Gospel,' 'a more effective way of preaching the Gospel' and on occasion 'just as good as the Gospel.' " (McGavran 1970: 36)

Fourth, the Church in many fields, for reasons known and unknown, did not experience much growth. Under such circumstances, it developed a defence and accepted a theology of mission which proclaimed that "only search" was God's command.

Being influenced by these four pressures, results in terms of men won for Christ have become suspect across wide stretches of the Church. They are seldom included as a goal of Christian mission. This has been a very unfortunate experience of the church bodies in Andhra. I could state at length that search theology is not pleasing to God, but here I make only one statement to indicate God's passion to find the lost.

Our Lord's parables emphasize an actual finding. In the fifteenth chapter of St. Luke, the woman does not merely search, but searches until she finds the lost coin. The shepherd does not make a token hunt; he makes a great effort to look for the lost sheep and finally finds it. If we look carefully, the Scriptures certainly provide us with the solution to get over the foggy thinking about the true mission of the Church.

I would like to present the New Testament pattern of evangelization toward which we Lutherans could with profit direct our steps. In what follows in the next five pages, I am greatly indebted to ideas from an article ("A New Testament Blueprint: Starting and Organizing Local Churches Overseas." Evangelical Missions Quarterly, (Fall) 1968: 28-37), by Vergil Gerber, missionary secretary of a Baptist Home Mission Society (CBFMS).

First of all, let us examine our Lord's commandment, regarding evangelization.

> But Jesus came and spoke these words to them, "All power in Heaven and on earth has been given to me, You, then, are to go and make disciples of all the nations and baptize them in the name of the Father and of the Son and of the Holy Spirit. Teach them to observe all that I have commanded you and remember, I am with you always, even to the end of the world." (Matthew 28: 19-20, Phillips' translation)

The following four things are included in the commission:

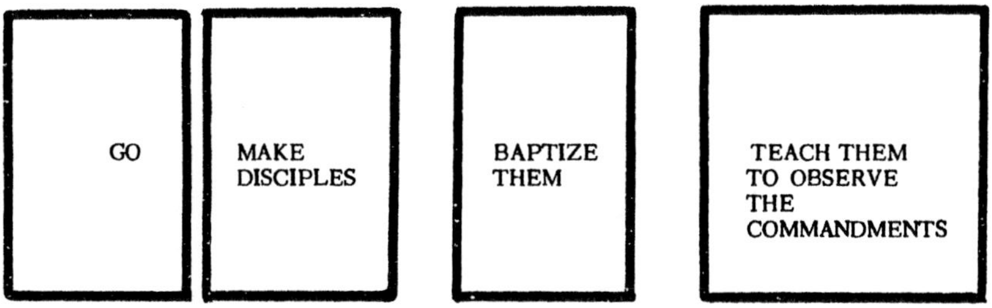

Our goal is to plant churches in all the communities. Fulfillment of the missionary mandate is to be measured in terms of church dimension.

To be an effective Christian, it is not enough to be an individual believer.

Elton Trueblood says:

> Men are never really effective unless they share in some kind of group reality. Inadequate as the fellowship of the church may be, in many generations, including our own, there is not the slightest chance of Christian vitality without it. New life normally arises from inside. (1969: 28)

Church growth theory puts emphasis on church planting in every community as the means to preach the Gospel to every creature. Each hamlet or locality really "hears" the Gospel best from its own members. We do not listen to what outsiders say nearly as much as to what our own people say. Thus, a church in the Reddys section of a village will have far more effect on Reddys than any outsider preaching in that village.

The Church is both the goal and the agent of dynamic reproduction. We find the best example in the Book of Acts, chapter 2. On the day of Pentecost, 3000 people were added to the fellowship of 120 who formed the first church in Jerusalem. Day after day they met in the temple; they broke bread together in their homes; shared meals with simple joy. These baptized members in turn reached out into the community gaining favour with people. Day after day the Lord added to their number people who were being saved.

Acts 2

They gladly received the Word v. 41	They were bap- tized v. 41	They were added to the Church v. 41	They were instructed by the Church v. 42	They reached out into the v. 47	They grew in numbers daily v. 47

This mission to reproduce herself in every nation is the dominant motif of the Book of the Acts. The promise of the Spirit is specifically to enable the disciples to be witnesses.

> But you are to be given power when the Holy Spirit has come to you. You will be witnesses to me, not only in Jerusalem, not only throughout Judea, not only in Samaria, but to the very ends of the earth! (Acts 1:8, Phillips' translation)

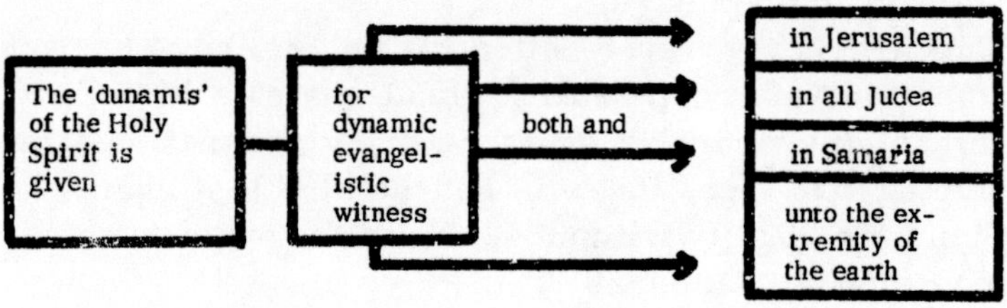

> 'The Great Commission derives its meaning and power wholly and exclusively from the Pentecost event.' 'Restlessly the spirit drives the church to witness, and continually churches rise out of witness.' Dynamic living cells multiply into hundreds of congregations in Asia, Europe, Africa, and around the world. (Trueblood 1969:29,30)

Dr. Gerber mentions two truths which lay the foundation for starting and organizing local churches. First of all, one must recognize the fact that only God can do this. "I will build my church and the gates of hell shall not prevail against it." (Matthew 16:18) This is the Spirit's ministry.

However, God has chosen men to build His Church. "God's methods are men, and we are the men! Melvin Hodges affirms, 'Methods are no better than the men behind them:

and men are no better than their contact with God.' " (Trueblood 1969: 30)

There is great need for the men themselves to be reminded of the truth that they should wholly depend upon the Spirit for constant power and guidance in order to have success in this great task of building churches. Incidentally, when I say building the church I do not mean the building of brick or stone at all. Dr. Gerber is also very particular not to put focus on the physical building. On the 24th of February, 1970, I had an interview with him. He said people are his main concern, church structures and the organization follow after the pattern of believers. He believes that discipling the nations is the main function of the missions. I wish all Christians and mission agencies would adopt this attitude which is so deeply scriptural.

Going back to the New Testament pattern of evangelization, three things come through with remarkable clarity in the pages of the New Testament which are essential for the Christianization of the people of Andhra Pradesh. They are well-defined mission, well-defined methods, and well-trained men.

Well-defined MISSION	Well-planned METHODS	Well-trained MEN

Well-Defined Mission

On the day of Pentecost (Acts 2), we see a responsible church growing out of witness. The first Christians were filled with the Holy Spirit and communicated the Gospel effectively. Men from all the nations received their witness. As a result, three thousand were baptized and added to the Jerusalem fellowship. Many others carried the Gospel to foreign lands.

The Holy Spirit	effectively communicated His message	through human witness	resulting in numerical reproduction	and geographical expansion

What clearly emerges is a newborn church with all the characteristics of what Beyerhaus and LeFever call "Responsible selfhood." From its inception individual and corporation responsibility can be seen in

ORGANIZING	They were immediately baptized and added to the new fellowship	v. 41
EDUCATING	They continued in the teaching of the Apostles	v. 42
SHARING	They sold their possessions to take care of their material needs	v. 45
REPRODUCING	They gained favor with all the people and the Lord added daily people who were being saved.	v. 47

"This self-determining and self-continuing nature of the Jerusalem church gives striking evidence of well-defined mission." (Trueblood 1969: 32)

Well-Planned Methods

Paul's methods were directly related to his predetermined mission. All of his missionary activity contributed to that end goal. "His was no vague effort to meet universal need which so often inspires what we loosely call 'evangelism,'" says McLeish. He concentrated on the creation and care of churches. (Trueblood 1969: 32,33)

In a short time, St. Paul was able to establish many churches and equip them with an ordained ministry. St. Paul selected natural leaders approved by their group, and committed them to the power and sufficiency of the Holy Ghost, ordaining them within a short time after their baptism. Most of them worked as honorary presbyters. In this way, from the beginning local churches were self-supporting and self-propagating. In my mind's eye, I can see thousands of such leaders all across my beloved Andhra.

Paul's carefully planned methods for starting and organizing churches concentrated on the synagogue communities. Because these were always found in great cities, the cities became his target. But his strategy was always to concentrate on the areas of greatest potential for church growth. He took time needed to plant churches and saw that they were taken care of by good Christian leaders.

> The simplicity of church government in New Testament practice is not accidental. As J.B. Phillips says, "This surely is the church as it was meant to be. It is vigorous and flexible, for these are the days before it ever became fat and short of breath through prosperity, or muscle-bound by over organization. (Trueblood 1969: 34)

Gustav Arneck (1834-1910), who has been called the founder of the scientific study of missionary principles, distinguishes three stages in the process of building a responsible church.

STAGE 1	STAGE 2	STAGE 3
Gathering of individual believers	Forming them into congregations	Joining of local congregations into a communion

In the twentieth century, many mission agencies look for a building almost as the first step in the development of a church, even before the preaching of the Gospel. The New Testament places no emphasis upon a building as the necessary means to the formation of a church. The Greek word ---ekklesia---literally means "called out ones" and is used in the Scriptures to denote the assembly of believers meeting together in a certain place or the designation of a specific fellowship of believers in a particular place.

> There is no clear example of a separate building set apart for Christian worship within the limits of the Roman empire before the third century. Paul concentrated his efforts not on buildings but on men. Men are God's method. (Trueblood 1969: 35)

Well-Trained Men

Our Lord selected his disciples with utmost care and they were willing to learn. The genius of His method is that He concentrated His teaching on these few. In the same way, Paul concentrated on potential leaders. In Andhra, we must concentrate on the thousands of yet to be discovered leaders of new congregations in unnumbered villages. I deal with the leadership training in detail in another chapter. "While great stress today is laid on money and methods, men are still God's means of reproducing responsible churches." (Trueblood 1969: 36)

The Unnecessary Offences. According to Scripture, we may legitimately ask those who become Christians to accept what the Saviour has done for them. This, natural man finds difficult. He likes to believe that he is saved by his own merits. To become a disciple of the Lord Jesus, a man must thus accept "the offence of the cross." This is a Scriptural offence. The evangelist cannot omit this and the believer cannot avoid it. Evangelization requires only the offence of the cross. But in Andhra Pradesh, we are making it very difficult and almost impossible for the caste people to become Christians by putting unscriptural offences in their way. For example, we compel them to join the church of another homogeneous unit. To quote Seamands:

> McGavran points out that any given society is made up of a number of subsocieties or subcultures. Society is not a uniform wall with one color of paint: it is, rather, a mosaic of different colors and patterns. Each subsociety has a character of its own; it ripens or becomes responsive at a different time; it develops a church of its own. (Seamands 1966: 25)

In the present situation, any caste person who becomes a Christian is identified with the Harijans and he is considered to be dead to his family and to his own community. Let us see in the experience of Narayan Vaman Tilak how much agony can be caused to the kith and kin where a person joins the "untouchable church." Mr. Tilak, the famous Marathi poet, was a convert from a high caste. After a long struggle, he was baptized but this was like news of death to his wife.

> The news of his baptism spread like wild fire on all sides. It was heard at once in Nasik. All his friends and relatives began to come in a steady stream to see my brother-in-law, Pendse, but in the house they sat in silence and no one said a word about it. Some of them would turn towards me and Dattu, screw up their faces and wipe their eyes. When I saw this pantomime, I fell into an indescribable state of mind. I wondered if Tilak had been killed in some terrible accident. (Tilak, Lakshmibai, 1956: 39,40)

Lakshmibai Tilak had a terrible shock on hearing about her husband's conversion which resulted in separation from the family. She made desperate attempts to die.

> Many and many a time in the next five years, I was on the point of taking my life, but I believe it was never possible. It was characteristic of me to grope on through the darkness of despair, but still to keep to the road. It was not in me to lie down and die half-way, but rather to rebound like a rubber ball. (Tilak, Lakshmibai, 1956: 42,43)

This has been the experience of many a convert. I know many friends who left their families and friends on account of Christianity. Of course, we take consolation in Scripture portions like Matthew 10: 37-38

> Anyone who puts his love for father or mother above his love for me does not deserve to be mine. and he who loves son or daughter more than me is not worthy of me, and neither is the man who refuses to take up his cross and follow my way. (Phillips' translation)

By this kind of approach, we might win one person here and one person there; but usually, the rest of his or her family and community turn hostile to Christ. Moreover, knowing the consequences, are we justified to suggest that they must join our existing Church only? If converts form a real Church of members of their own community, is not this costly decision equally agreeable to God?

I believed and still believe that the body of Christ is casteless, but to make it as a precondition for an individual to accept the Lord seems to me to be unscriptural. And by putting undue emphasis on the caste issue, we are pleading more for social change than for spiritual conversion. Maybe we are on par with social reformers and politicians whose ultimate goal is to bring about social uplift. By and large, in Andhra and also in other parts of India, conversion is misunderstood as a shift from one homogeneous unit to another. It is commonly said, "You have joined the outcastes."

Jesus said, "He who believes and is baptized will be saved, he who believes not is condemned." But some of us are adding, "He who believes and is baptized in a particular church will be saved." This certainly is an unnecessary offence we are putting in the way of those who would accept the Saviour. What God desires is to reconcile men to Himself through Jesus Christ in the Church of Jesus Christ. Since it is immaterial whether someone joins an outcaste church or caste church, we should permit those who desire to do so to join congregations made up of their own kind.

But unfortunately, it became tradition in churches in Andhra to expect people to join the existing congregations. The consensus of opinion is that the Scriptures demand it. Contrary to this, St. Paul says:

> For though I am no man's slave, yet I have made myself everyone's slave, that I might win more men to Christ. To the Jews I was a Jew that I might win the Jews. To those who were under the law I put myself in the position of being under the law (although in fact, I stand free of it), that I might win those who are under the law. (I Corinthians 9: 19-20, Phillips)

Paul did not expect anyone to change to suit his (Paul's) convenience; rather as the ambassador of Christ he became all things to all men. Whereas in our situation, we want to see the fruits of the Spirit in these caste people even before they become Christians and thus demand that they leave their people in order to be Christians.

Bishop Newbigin certainly indicates that there should not be any social barrier for the Hindus to become Christians:

> I would encourage a believing Hindu to become a Christian. I will not say to him: Become one of us, a Christian like me and follow all the habits and customs you see among the people called Christians. (1969: 110)

In this profound statement, we can find the Christian solution to the problem. As Bishop Newbigin points out, we appeal to a Hindu for the change of faith, but not for the change of community. He can be a Christian where he is.

My third questionnaire was answered by thirty-five missionaries who work in twenty-six countries and represent eleven different denominations. To my first question, "Is it Scriptural to start separate churches (worship places) for caste converts?" all said "yes" basing their answer on the Holy Bible.

It is necessary and advantageous to have separate congregations for converts for the promotion of the Gospel.

The Advantages of Separate Congregations

I am advocating separate congregations for converts from new ethnic units. Some may object that in one town or village there should be only one church. It is however highly likely that the Jerusalem Church of 5,000 men (and perhaps 15,000 additional women and children) met for prayer, instruction, and "breaking bread" (Acts 2:42) in many separate congregations.

Furthermore, after noticing the peculiar needs of the caste section of the population, I hope readers will be convinced of the reasonableness and need of starting separate congregations for converts from these sections. This need has been recognized by Rev. S. W. Schmitthenner who advocated special parishes for Sudhras.

> This proposal is that we have a special parish ministry for Sudhras. We already have a special evangelistic ministry to them. but we have seen that as a whole the Sudhra Christians are neglected, and that they need frequent visits and concerned shepherding. Therefore, we should have special parishes, made up of Sudhra prayer groups which are already established, with an evangelistic pastor whose full-time responsibility is to shepherd these small congregations and to work through them to start new Sudhra congregations and to bring in new members. (Schmitthenner 1968: 29)

Pastor Schmitthenner is the president of the Andhra Evangelical Lutheran Church. His years as district evangelistic missionary and his survey of the entire field convinced him that such special parishes are necessary.

It is most gratifying that the Executive Council of the Lutheran Church accepted Mr. Schmitthenner's plan to have three special evangelistic parishes for Sudhras, and implemented it from June 1, 1969.*

To disciple Hindus, it is most essential to form congregations in their midst. The nucleus groups of converts now existing will serve as pioneers for the proclamation of the Gospel among Hindus and thus prepare the way for the rest of the community to become Christians. Under the present system---where converts have to propose to their relatives that they become Christians in another ethnic unit---there is very little possibility for the caste community to accept Jesus Christ as Guru and Saviour.

Usually baptism is presented as necessary for membership. But of the many that hear and wish to accept the Gospel, very few find it possible to accept a baptism which so thoroughly identifies them with another community in the neighbourhood.

A few do accept baptism. These, however, feel they have done the ultimate, are satisfied with themselves, and do not go any further. Baptism which should be the beginning of the Christian life becomes the end of it. Having surmounted the huge hurdle of baptism in what they believe to be the Harijan Church, converts feel there is little else to do in the matter.

True, a few exceptionally earnest converts have the enthusiasm to participate in the programme of the Church, but since they live some distance away from the rest of the congregation they are unable to take a vigorous part in this programme.

....

*"Special Committee on evangelism parishes. Implementation plan: Rev. S.W. Schmitthenner, Chairman. (1) Voted that the following plan be adopted in implementing the evangelistic parishes in the Synods." Extract from the Church records. (Ref. LCM 148/473)

In the Indian tradition, women do not have much freedom to make their own decision to attend church. This is especially the case when the family is not in favour of their being Christians. So even the few who are baptized in Andhra find it very difficult to be a part of the congregation made up of members of other ethnic units. For want of fellowship and Christian nurture, they can neither grow spiritually nor be effective witnesses.

In spite of all these handicaps, there are to be sure converts because of whose fervent faith others are brought to the Lord. The reader can imagine how wonderful it will be for the discipling of the receptive homogeneous units of my people if arrangements are made for these glowing converts to have churches in their own communities. They can then bring their loved ones to Christ without requiring that they cross cultural and ethnic barriers.

Non-Christian relatives and friends can hear the Gospel while the converts worship and witness right in the midst of their kith and kin. If it is a rural area, the whole village will have an opportunity to know what Christianity is. I believe this is both the New Testament and the natural way of communicating the Gospel. If there is enough flexibility and freedom in our approach to Hindus, house churches will grow naturally among them.

House Churches are Scriptural

House churches were most common in Biblical times. Indeed, for the first hundred years, most churches were house churches. Floyd V. Filson writes an exhaustive account of "the significance of the early house churches." Basing his comments on Scriptural evidence, he says that house churches were in existence from the very first days of the Church. When the Christians wanted to meet as Christians, the homes of the members suited them best. As they grew in number, they divided themselves into different groups and met in separate houses. Filson makes the following statement that, when Christians multiplied in number,

> It became increasingly difficult for all the believers in the city to meet in one house. For all ordinary

> occasions, at least, the total body would split into smaller groups which could be housed in private homes . . . the house church dominated the situation . . . the regular setting for both Christian meetings and evangelistic preaching was found in the homes of believers . . . a study of home churches furthers understanding of the apostolic church (in five ways). The house church enabled the followers of Jesus to have a distinctively Christian worship and fellowship from the very first days of the apostolic age . . . (They) afford a partial explanation of the great attention paid to family life in the letters of Paul . . . The existence of several house churches (congregations) in one city goes far to explain the tendency to party strife in the apostolic age . . . A study of the house church . . . also throws light on the social status of the early Christians . . . the development of church polity can never be understood without reference to the house churches. . . (1939: 106)

As the Christian movement spread around the Mediterranean Sea, the same development occurred in all places. When the synagogue was closed to Christians (as it was soon after the first few became Christians), the house church played an important role. Occasionally, as we see in Acts 19:9, when the synagogue shut the Christians out, they went to a public lecture hall. Since the record says this went on "for two years," we may be sure that after that the Christians of Ephesus turned to house churches, the regular setting for both worship and evangelistic preaching was likely to be found in the homes of the believers.

Let me give a few of the many examples of house churches mentioned in the New Testament. Priscilla and Aquila made their home a centre of Christian fellowship and teaching. "Greetings from the Churches of Asia. Aquila and Priscilla send you their warmest Christian greetings and so does the Church that meets in their house." (I Corinthians 16:19, Phillips' translation)

There is a specific mention of a prayer meeting in the house of Mary, the mother of John Mark in Acts 12:12. Even when house churches are not specifically mentioned, we can infer them. Thus, the epistle to the Hebrews seems to have been addressed to believers meeting in house churches. The "Italians" mentioned may well have been a house church of Christians from that ethnic unit (cf. 10:25, 13:24).

A study of the Acts and epistles reveals that the chief place where believers are said to have held their regular meetings was the home. About twenty times, we read of Christians carrying out their united worship in the home of a believer. Four times "the Church in the house" is specifically mentioned (Romans 16:5; I Corinthians 16:19; Colossians 4:15; and Philemon 2).

House Churches in Andhra

The house church system works well in Andhra. Later on, when congregations grow bigger, converts will no doubt want to build specials houses for worship. This has been their way of doing things in Hinduism.

In the month of June 1969, I was in my village (Bodipalem) for three weeks and was much impressed with the zeal of the Hindus. They were meeting daily for worship. (They call it bhajana.) They have no paid leaders or professional priests. Their leaders arise in a natural way out of the situation. When these fine people accept Christ, they may confidently be expected to worship Him even more fervently.

Bhajanas led by Kammas, Reddys, and Kapus constitute a new departure in Hinduism. Previously, my people gave more importance to the temple and the priest, and the priest was always a Brahmin.

In recent years, Brahmin dominance greatly diminished. Sudhras are practicing what Christians call "the priesthood of all believers" in thousands of house gatherings. I have been closely associated with these, for my brother is one of the leaders.

The following is their usual pattern of worship. About seven o'clock in the evening after dinner, men, women and children start coming to a central place. No bells are rung. Though most do not have watches or clocks in their houses, gathering is rapid. The observer will be surprised to see how soon they assemble. The first ones to arrive start singing accompanied by their simple musical instruments like wooden clappers, tambourines, and bells. In a short time, hundreds gather around one of the members who has a large house and a large open yard. Of course, the house owner has invited the group "to have a bhajana" at his house. The many worshippers streaming to that house form a kind of procession. They go singing to that house and spend at least two hours there. Evening after evening, they keep doing it this way.

The bhajana I am describing happened to be right in front of our house and for those three weeks, I was there and watched this great event with much interest. I also experimented by starting a Christian version of this bhajana in our house on a small scale. My nephews and nieces became much interested and brought their friends to participate in the informal event.

Sometimes my brother---leader of his own Hindu bhajana ---stayed with us participating in our Christian bhajana and did not attend nearby Hindu bhajanas. But since he is a leading person, often somebody came and took him over to the other gathering.

Later I tried out this kind of programme at our ashram. Many attended and like this natural way of praising God.

The Advantages of House Churches

If we want to communicate the Gospel in a natural way and in an effective manner, house churches---at least in Andhra among the caste communities---are the fitting means. House churches have many advantages: (a) Hindus are used to this kind of fellowship and worship. (b) If the same system is Christianized, they feel quite at home in it and participate easily in it. (c) This is most important for the spiritual life of the members. The Word of the Lord in hymns and Bible passages gets through to them. (d) Meeting in the home avoids much of the unreality fostered by putting on special clothes to go to hear the Gospel in a "church building" in the residential quarters of an ethnic unit which they consider very different to their own.

(e) Through house churches, we demonstrate Christianity in the midst of the non-Christian community. Each new house exposes a new set of intimates and relatives. In Andhra, when any religious programme goes on in the neighbourhood, crowds are certain to attend it. As in the days of Jesus and in apostolic times, these crowds will be composed of all kinds of persons. Whatever might be their attitude toward the Christian religion, they will have an opportunity to witness a Christian congregation of their own kind of people and to listen to the Word of God coming to them over the lips of their own kith and kin. In this way, the Holy Spirit can work in their very hearts unhindered by any strange witness or flavour of foreignness.

We do not expect them to change overnight. Since the church is in their neighbourhood, the Hindu public will be involuntarily thrown into a Christian environment. The converts can exercise their faith in many ways for the advantage of their neighbours. Even now, where there are "prayer cells" in caste areas, many Hindus are attracted to the prayer and fellowship.

In Sri Rangapatnam, a village about twenty-five miles away from Rajahmundry, one convert woman has a regular worship service in her house. When she was a Hindu, she used one of the large rooms in her house as a worship place for her many Hindu gods. After she became a Christian, she converted that room into a prayer room. I was much impressed with the way she kept it. The Bible, songbooks, and wooden cross are always there. She spreads mats on the floor for people to kneel on in prayer. Daily she has devotions there, maybe with a few on weekdays; but on Sunday a large number gathers. On Friday, several caste people---Christians and Hindus---fast and keep vigil the whole night. In the last few years, the whole neighbourhood came to know about Jesus Christ. From that one village, over fifty people attended our Christian ashram.

At one time, I questioned this Christian lady asking her whether she had any objection to go to what her neighbours called "the Harijan Church" for Sunday worship. I shall never forget her reply. She said that for her own spiritual benefit she would be glad to go to the Church, but if she did so, many of her Hindu intimates who worship with her would be deprived of the privilege of praying to the Lord Jesus Christ. It is true. If she wants she can attend the existing church building about 200 yards from her house in the Harijan residential area. She is a rich and elderly woman and her family puts no obstacle in the way of her practicing Christianity. But she deeply desires to bring the Gospel to her many friends and relatives and her house is a church for them. It is my conviction that she is doing right and her experiment should be deliberately multiplied.

In another village, Athili, several converts made their houses into prayer centres. One of the Gospel workers in our church, Devakarunamna, helped (and still helps) to conduct prayers on Sunday at these centres. I was there in October, 1968, and the Christians certainly appreciated these services. The many Hindu friends who participate in these services are richly blessed in Christian experience. Just imagine how much will be the outreach if we start many such house churches and deliberately honour and emphasize them all over Andhra province.

Another important factor is that the expenses incurred in the building and upkeep of large church buildings are saved. Since we cannot expect Hindus to build large churches before they know the Lord or experience the Gospel, the house church which they can patronize before baptism seems a reasonable procedure.

Moreover, for the mission or the existing Church to invest money in buildings in caste sections may not be a wise thing to do. Especially in these pioneer projects, that money can be used for many other things which are essential for communicating of the Gospel.

If we have a church building, it will be just in one area. Without any cash outlay, house churches provide as many places to worship as there are groups of converts. And Hindus in each immediate area will have the benefit of that particular house church. In this way, house churches can open to the Church many new valuable avenues of advance.

Existing churches are places for the nurture of Christians only. In other words, they are "shut in churches," whereas house churches have doors open to non-Christians to worship with those of our friends who have yet to believe in Jesus as Christ the Saviour.

I know Hindus love to participate in our church services. Many of my Hindu friends and relatives go to church on some Sundays and on special occasions like Christmas. It is worth listening to their joyous experiences. But because of the social barriers which sadly but inevitably surround existing churches, it is not possible for them to do it often.

Even converts with great desire to worship with Harijan Christians find it difficult to go all the way to the palem. Their families and friends plead with them not to bring shame on them all by identifying with Harijans in worship. Moreover, in some areas of Andhra, as we have seen in our church, we have more women converts. Their husbands and brothers do not allow them to go by themselves.

I remember how deeply my family and relatives were hurt when I first went to "the church." My grandmother even came to the church and when she saw me sitting along with other Christians (all of them Harijans by background), she could not tolerate it and pleaded with me publicly to have my devotions in my own house. My relatives taunted me constantly and called me an outcaste.

Note that Hindus often do not object to a person's believing in the Lord Jesus and praying to Him. The great obstacle is joining a church of a despised segment of Hindu society.

At the risk of repeating myself, let me say that I have no desire to perpetuate caste exclusiveness and caste pride. My people are wrong in their attitude toward the existing churches and existing Christians. But merely to say this does no good. The question is how to change this sinful attitude. The best way is not---I am certain--- to force every new Christian to convert culturally in order to join a church made up of Christians of another ethnic unit. The way is to smooth the path which leads to joyful Christian discipleship. The way is to lead hundreds of thousands of India's fine sons and daughters to accept the Bible as their rule of faith and practice. Separate Sudhra congregations will help this occur naturally. That is why I advocate them as a provisional and temporary measure, a step in the right direction.

The reader should observe that I am not advocating the abandonment of biblical standards. I am advocating rather the considerable adaptions of European and American forms* to make them fit the sociological realities of Andhra.

The separatism which I propose must be understood as temporary and provisional. It is merely a stage in a long journey. In the beginning, a certain amount of freedom and flexibility is needed to try out or explore various ways and means to disciple Hindus. After enough of them are converted, the stigma of Christianity being an "outcast" religion will disappear. Then there will be greater possibility for Christian unity.

I am a firm believer in the Church universal and the brotherhood of man. The long range goal must be full brotherhood with full equality of opportunity. But, let it be remembered that this is "in Christ." It happens only after one comes into the Lord. The existing churches have demanded the fruits of the Spirit in non-Christians before they receive the Spirit. In my own experience, I know how bitter I was towards Harijan Christians before I became a Christian. When I accepted the Lord, a miracle happened. My whole attitude changed and I felt, and still feel, one with them in like precious faith.

As congregations multiply---thousands of them---among many caste communities, they will do many things in common with the existing churches which will build up the unity of the Church. Common theological training will help all church leaders to have the same faith and the same doctrinal foundation. Youth and women's programmes can be the same for all. Common communion services will, of course, be arranged occasionally. We can also celebrate some festivals like Christmas together.

A few years ago, I witnessed Christmas at Revendrapad (a village near Guntur) where converts and Harijan Chris-

*That these alien forms have been accepted by the existing Indian Church---which represents only a very small part of the total Indian heritage---does not mean that they are representative Indian forms.

tians joyously celebrated our Lord's birth. In this village, about twenty Kamma families became Christian and they have a church building in their midst. Harijan Christians have a small prayer shed. They came over to the church in the village and we all had wonderful fellowship and worship. This can happen in many places.

Our ashram programme aims at dissolving communal differences. Hindus have certain peculiar ways of looking at things. When they go on a pilgrimage, they do not observe caste rules. They regard it as an exception and associate themselves with anybody. In just the same way, they consider an ashram a place of pilgrimage and gladly live together. We have already experienced this close sisterhood in our ashram.

Thinking of the unity of the church, I venture to say that if congregations are started in the villages, they can be melting points for the differences between the two Harijan community churches in the palems. These two sections of the Church now feel neither is ready to give in. The church in the village might help both to forget their differences. In the providence of God, all might in practice become one as both are now one in theory.

I see this as a real possibility because I observed something of this sort happening in my own village. The two Harijan communities are on either side of the village. They worship separately and do not eat together. In the last few years, however, educated Hindu friends invited candidates from both sections of the community for fellowship and dinner. Both of them came and to the surprise of many, everybody ate together.

Since Hindus are an overwhelming majority in Andhra villages, when they are convinced of the Christian principles---when Christ dwells in their hearts through faith---differences will disappear and we can very well hope for Christian unity. But we cannot attain these valuable fruits of the Spirit even over centuries, if we do not give the non-Christians freedom to accept the Lord in their own culture.

It is true our Lord desires Christian unity, but as Dr. Gibbard has said, unity for the sake of unity is not enough. In his recent visit to South India, Dr. Gibbard Mark of Great

Britain made a survey in the Church of South India. In his book entitled Unity is not Enough, he made the following statement:

> In almost every congregation I went to I asked 'What are you doing about mission?' nearly always the answer was, 'We send money for our CSI (Church of South India) missionary in Thailand,' and sometimes, 'We have each year a week of evangelism, or we organize an area evangelistic convention.' And when I went on to ask, 'What difference is your congregation making to your village or your town?' the answer usually was a puzzled silence. (1965: 104)

In a country like India, where over 97 per cent of the population is non-Christian, we will not be justified by aiming merely for the organizational union of existing churches. The Great Commission constantly reminds us of the concern of our Lord for discipling the nations (ta ethne—the castes and tribes, the ethnic units). Our efforts should be directed towards this primary goal. The establishment of house churches will result in a far greater number of Christians and the unity of the church can eventually be attained.

Each house church thrusts the responsibilities and prestige of leadership on several able men and women. When the group grows too large for the house, it can divide into two homes, and these two groups can divide again and yet again. Thus the Church grows and expands rapidly over a much larger area. Along with it, leaders develop from among the members themselves. The Holy Spirit can freely work without being limited by the amount of subsidy which until now has been needed by highly trained professional ministers. When the whole Church grows strong and numerous, then subsidy from the West will be diminished and probably eliminated. A highly trained ministry is no doubt needed; but as the Gospel spreads among the caste people it must also depend on numerous lay leaders. Training these unpaid persons is tremendously important.

The leaders ministering to small groups in homes would overcome much of the temptation to self-importance which ruins so much of God's work where large buildings and a big congregation are involved. The house church leader will be a spiritual leader without being involved in "big administration and big politics."

House churches will be composed of small groups in the friendly associations of a home. Every Christian can know everybody else---and many non-Christians also---and thus relationships are more real and less formal. With limited numbers in each house congregation, it is possible for everybody to take an active part in the worship service and other activities. Thus the whole body of Christ can function effectively.

The Function of the House Churches

The house churches I am proposing to have for converts will have the same status as the New Testament house churches.

> The early Church was taught to regard themselves not merely as a collection of saved individuals, but as active members of the Body of Christ. Not only did all believers form the one Body universal but each group functioned as the Body locally. In each of the three cases where these are mentioned (Romans 12, I Corinthians 12, and Ephesians 4), there is no suggestion of one man ministering to the whole group, but each is shown as having the privilege of possessing some spiritual gift, and the responsibility to minister this gift to the rest of the local church, so that every believer is looked on as a minister to the rest. (Pethybridge, n.d.: 7)

Since we believe in the "priesthood of all believers," how well this fits into the Lutheran pattern. The picture we have of the Early Church is very simple. I am glad is is not as complicated as that of the present day Church. Whenever "two or three gathered together" in the name of the Lord, there they expected to find the risen Lord present in their midst. They also expected His Spirit to work in each of them. Thus the emphasis was not on the ministry of a particular individual. With this kind of understanding of the Scriptures, Luther pronounced the great doctrine to be "priesthood of all believers."

According to Acts 2:46, they were "breaking bread from house to house." It is clearly stated that the Christians celebrated the Lord's Supper in their homes. In Andhra when we think of the house churches, we must think of having communion and baptism also in those churches.

During Bible times, it appears that some houses were built with a large upper room. When our Lord used such a room, there is no mention of that room being "dedicated" or especially set apart. In fact, the whole emphasis of the New Testament is that "God's temple" is the individual believer, the local church and the Church universal rather than any building constructed by human hands.

For the good of evangelization in Andhra, let us act in accordance with this Biblical pattern rather than along the lines of mere human tradition. We can be quite confident of God's blessing on our programme of house churches. The concerned leaders of these congregations should administer the sacraments like baptism and communion. The details of leadership will be discussed in Chapter VI.

Home Communions in the United States of America

My suggestion of having the Lord's Supper in the house churches is based on the Scriptures and is also in line with recent thinking and practice in advanced countries like the United States of America.

In the month of December, 1969, I had the pleasure of visiting two retired Lutheran missionaries (Miss R. H. Swanson and Miss M. Meissner). Both are keen Christians and have given long and fruitful years of service in Andhra. I interviewed them on the 18th and 19th of December regarding the communion service in their church (Christ Lutheran Church, San Lorenzo, California). Miss Swanson told me about the home communions they are having and Miss Meissner shared with me her experience in an informal communion service entitled "The Table of the Lord." She said that she appreciated this new experience.

Home communions were set up on a zone basis and zone captains called members to them. Between September 19 and October 6, 1969, seventeen home communions were celebrated in this one congregation. Miss Swanson said they appreciated these home communions and she wrote "We seemed to experience a deeper sense of fellowship one with another."

By having home communions and other types of informal communion services, Christ Lutheran Church is trying to practice the simple procedures of the Early Church and to get at the real meaning of Holy Communion.

I myself participated in an informal communion service in the Deaconess Home, Philadelphia, in the month of August, 1969. Many ministers in America are discouraged by the small amount of truth members of their congregations are able to absorb simply by sitting in the pew listening to messages from the pulpit. So they are making attempts, through home communions and in other ways, to get the members involved in the service.

Unity in Diversity

Some might wonder how the unity of the Church is maintained in this programme of numerous house churches. The writer certainly believes in the Church universal and in church unity. She understands that for the first 200 years after Christ, the Church did not have any special buildings. As each house congregation increased in membership, it divided into a number of groups and these continued in fellowship with each other. All the small gatherings in a particular town or village would together form "the Church of God in Ephesus," or wherever it might be.

In this way, there was unity in the Early Church and the same is possible in Andhra. The introduction of separate congregations for Hindus need not and must not affect the unity of the Church. In towns like Rajahmundry and Guntur, we have several Lutheran Churches in different geographical areas. These different parishes have their own separate worship services and carry on all parish activities separately. Still we all belong to the one Lutheran Church. In the same way, the churches for the converts will still be a part of the Andhra Evangelical Lutheran Church. Though Hans Kung was speaking to a different situation, his words apply also to our Andhra situation.

> As long as these churches recognize one another as legitimate, as long as they see one another as part of one and the same Church, as long as they are in fellowship with one another and hold common services, and especially celebrate the Eucharist together, and as long as they are helping one another, working together and standing together in times of difficulty and persecution, there can be no objection to their diversity. (1967:275)

Indigenous Churches

These separate congregations I am proposing must be indigenous churches from the beginning. Care must be taken to plant indigenous churches. Everyone knows that the Church in every land must be a church of that land and that culture. But what I am saying goes farther than that elementary truth. The church must be a church of each subculture. Freedom of each ethnic unit in each land to follow its own culture has to be recognized. In Andhra, not only must we have Indian churches, but also churches which fit the main subcultures and main ethnic units of this great province.

Since our concern is establishing churches among caste Hindus, it is most essential to constitute the congregations in the pattern familiar to them.

It is generally recognized that re-structure of the congregation is very important.

> In 1961 the World Council of Churches embarked on a long-term ecumenical study programme entitled "The Missionary Structure of the Congregation," the object of which was to discover how the Church could break out of its present irrelevant patterns and be reformed around the structure of the world's needs. (Barrett 1968: 172)

The re-structure I am proposing is not merely of the kind that Dr. Barrett is talking about. It is much more important. The present structure of our Andhra churches is not suited to multiplying congregations among caste Hindus. Bearing this in mind, a new and best possible procedure should be adopted for structuring congregations in the new social areas.

Churches which are really indigenous to the ethnic units I am concerned about will have a structure different from that of the existing churches among the landless labourers of this province. What does it mean to be really indigenous?

John Nevius expounded the indigenous church principles which have come to be known all around the world. The following are his six principles. I follow closely the statement of them set forth in Understanding Church Growth. (McGavran 1970: 337,339)

First, let each convert abide in the calling wherein he was called (I Corinthians 7:20). Each continues to earn his living as he did before he became a Christian and to live where he did before he was baptized.

Second, trust unpaid lay leaders---elders and teachers--- to shepherd the little flock. "The characteristic feature of our churches is that the principal care of them is entrusted not to paid preachers set over them and resident among them, but to unpaid leaders belonging to the churches."

Third, let churches meet in the homes of the members, or let them build meeting houses on their level, belonging to them.

Fourth, let the churches be supervised by paid evangelists or helpers and by the missionary himself. Nevius baptized about 1,000 persons and lost (by reversion and excommunication) about 200. The remaining 800 constituted sixty churches, i.e. there were about a dozen members to a church. One paid worker supervised another ten.

Fifth, give extensive training to the unpaid leaders and to all Christians. Nevius had a month-long Bible training class at the mission station (200 miles distance from the village house churches). During this month, he gave intensive training to the leaders and tried to get the more advanced converts to attend. The Sunday service was chiefly teaching, not sermonized. Instruction of catechumen was done by the unpaid local leaders.

Sixth, new churches are planted by the existing churches. (How well this would fit our situation! Existing groups of converts would plant new churches among their own ethnic unit!) As Christians earn their living and visit their friends and kinsmen in a web of relationship and acquaintance, they find new groups which are considering becoming Christians. Existing Christians teach these inquirers, the supervisor also instructs them occasionally, and when they are ready for examination and baptism, the missionary first sees them. (This last, of course, is not needed in modern India.) Thus churches multiply in a normal way.

Nevius' principles were tested and found to be good working tools. If we adopt these principles in all main subcultures in Andhra, we can be sure of having churches which are indigenous to each ethnic unit and self-propagating. As Dr. McGavran points out, indigenous churches grow better than others. He says (1970: 341-343):

> Natural witness by the whole membership becomes more possible. The naturalness of Christian life and worship, witness and learning, is what tells. "Unconscious" witness is perhaps the most potent element in growing churches . . .
>
> As congregations grow in size and increase in number, indigenous church principles would urge that Christians call full time pastors paid by the congregation (in that ethnic unit), not by the founding church in some other ethnic unit or mission. Church buildings too should be constructed as soon as possible, but by the Christians themselves, not by outside aid.

The Note of Urgency for the Establishment of Congregations Among Hindus

The situation in Andhra calls for much prayer and willingness to act more in accordance with Bible patterns and indigenous church principles than along lines of Western tradition. We need people like Luther with courage to adopt new and more effective means to expand God's Kingdom.

The Hindu-Christian Movement around K. Subbarao

In recent years, a movement around K. Subbarao has drawn the attention of Christians and non-Christians alike in Andhra.

Mr. Subbarao was born in Eluru in Godavari district fifty-eight years ago. He belongs to the Kamma caste, grew up in a Hindu home, but rebelled against the religion and the religious practices of his forefathers.

The origin of Subbarao's "Christian" movement goes back to the vision of Christ which its leader had in 1942. At that time, he was headmaster of a high school. When he was sick in the hospital he had a vision described in one of his Telugu poems. For a long time Mr. Subbarao told no one about the vision.

> It seems that he was ashamed to mention it, not only because he, an educated agnostic, should not believe in such things, but also because Jesus Christ to him was known as the God of the untouchables. Subbarao was proud of his caste, and he did not want to have anything to do with such a "god." (Baago, K. 1968: 5)

The quotation is taken from a pamphlet entitled "The Movement Around Subbarao" by Dr. Kaj Baago, formerly professor of Church History at the United Theological College, Bangalore. Dr. M. M. Thomas, now executive secretary of the Central Committee of the World Council of Churches, wrote a preface in which he says:

> The movement raises several theological questions for the Church . .
>
> It is here that the challenge to the very idea of the Church which Subbarao and Dr. Baago present is relevant to the Church in India. (Baago 1968: iii, iv)

In the above quotations, Dr. Thomas and Dr. Baago are drawing our attention to many important factors. One such is that the existing Lutheran Church has projected the image of Christ as "the god of the untouchables." Other denominations also have done this. This image is causing a mental block among countless Hindus to knowing and accepting Christ. The image causes an even greater block to accepting baptism in what Hindus consider "the Harijan Church."

Subbarao was influenced by this feeling right from the time of his vision. Because of it only, I believe he tried not to identify himself as a follower of Christ. But the miracles or strange happenings which began to take place when he prayed forced him to come out in the open.

In the name of the Lord Jesus, he heals the sick and drives out evil spirits. He follows a particular procedure when he exercises his healing ministry. As the word spread of Subbarao's power, the people of his own* and surrounding villages and towns came to him. Later on, people from distant parts of India also came. Now he is well known all over India. Many beg to visit him; among these are prominent business men and political leaders.

Dr. Baago, writing about Subbarao and the Church, makes the following statement.

> We have already mentioned that Subbarao originally regarded Christ as the "God of the untouchables." It is a fact that the Church in Andhra consists almost exclusively of "Harijans," and that any caste-Hindu there will find it almost impossible to become a member of the Church. (Baago 1968: 8)

Dr. M. M. Thomas rightly points out some implications of this difficult situation.

> The new converts should, therfore, be recognizable as the firstfruit for Christ of the society to which they belong, bringing their specific gifts into the fellowship. This means that the (existing) Church must not seek to impose its whole traditional style of life upon the new convert. We have to confess that because this has often been done in the past, baptism has been made to appear as an act by which a person repudiates his ancient cultural heritage and accepts an alien culture. (Baago 1968: 9)

Subbarao's movement is spreading greatly. A large number of people have become devotees of Christ through Subbarao's ministry.

> Subbarao claims to have had contacts with two or three hundred thousand people during the last ten years.
>
> The regular prayer meetings are quite simple in their structure. The first one which I attended was a fairly small gathering of about 30-40 people and took

*Munipalli is a place about fifteen miles from my own village. I have visited that village many times. B.V.S.

> place on the open veranda of the big house of a factory owner. The second one was larger, 100-150 people who sat under a pandal in a private garden. It should be noted that there was no attempt on the part of these Hindu devotees of Christ to conceal these meetings from neighbours and others. (Baago 1968: 11)

I am convinced of the fact that Subbarao and his followers want Christ, but not the existing Harijan Christian Church. This is the problem. One must ask why? Much could be said here; but rather than discuss possible reasons, I would like to present a simple solution: start congregations made up of converts from Hinduism right in the midst of the new ethnic units as I have described before and the whole problem will be solved.

Baago makes a great point of avoiding baptism altogether. This is neither necessary nor scriptural. Hindus have nothing against baptism. They are used to having special religious ceremonies and water is important in their worship service. The priest often pours water into the hands of the devotee who pours it on his own head. Sometimes the priest or guru sprinkles water on the head of the worshipper. There is almost no ceremony without the use of the water. For men living in such a culture, baptism in itself should be readily understood and desirable. But when "baptism" means "identifying oneself with Harijan Christians," it is highly objectionable.

Over the years, there have been many individuals and groups of individuals who accepted Christ but could not bring themselves to join the Church because of social barriers. Thus countless thousands of earnest potential Christians have been denied the privilege of becoming Christ's disciples and inheriting abundant and eternal life.

Dr. A. G. Hogg, who was professor in Madras Christian College in India, gives an excellent example of a young Brahmin student who received the Lord into his heart and even propagated the Gospel, but refused to have baptism. Every Sunday morning he used to gather a number of Hindus on the veranda of his house and preach Christ to them.

Dr. Hogg says:

> Presently I began to wonder whether I should raise

> with him the question of joining the Church by baptism I took counsel with a senior colleague, a man whose life and teaching I knew to be the most effective Christian influence in our College. In reply he asked me the question: "Do you think a Brahmin convert can be baptized and still continue to be a Christian"? I was not so inexperienced as to be unable to understand that seemingly paradoxical suggestion. It was not of the dangers of persecution that my colleague was thinking but of the perils of disillusionment. The Brahmin who undergoes baptism is cutting himself off from a community-life in which his whole development has been rooted. (1947: 40)

Being well educated and well informed about the social life of different communities in India, Dr. Hogg did not seem to feel it right to ask the young man to sacrifice his family and community ties. But he was beset with the great theological problem and says,

> Nevertheless, there is equal force in the counter question whether a convert can continue to be a Christian if he refuses to offer himself for baptism. (1947: 41)

This has been the dilemma from ages past and still is in the present. Dr. K. Rajaratnam of India makes the following statement:

> A situation unique to the Indian Church is the Nicodemus type of Christian, of whom there are large numbers. People who are prepared to listen to the Gospel who are inspired by its truth, who accept Christ as an Avatar (incarnation) of God, but who question the need for baptism. Some such "believers" are even preaching the Gospel and performing miracles in the name of Christ. (1970: 14)

Both Dr. Hogg and Dr. Rajaratnam, it seems to me, miss the true solution to the problem. It is no solution to permit or encourage a baptismless, churchless, unbiblical Christianity. The true solution is to do what the Bible requires: Be baptized in the name of the Father, Son and Holy Spirit. Confess Christ openly before men. Become a full member of His Body, the Church. Have fellowship with all other members of The Body. Accept the Bible as the authoritative Word of God. But at the same time, recognize that the church in each language group, each culture and sub-culture, each main ethnic unit should be allowed and encouraged to grow in that language group, that sub-culture, that ethnic unit. Brotherhood will come, It is a fruit of the Spirit. It is not and never must be made to be a pre-condition of baptism.

The central question is this: Shall we let these seeking, receptive Hindus, these beloved relatives of mine, become Christians in their own culture and in their own neighbourhoods? To do so is very right and very urgent.

If we delay too long, many "Hindu-Christian" movements will arise and take all kinds of strange forms. Which do we prefer to see: Our Hindu converts as fellow Christians in a separate congregation of our orthodox Churches, or "Hindu-Christians" as hostile members of strange denominations of syncristic and heretical nature without baptism, without church, and without the Bible as sole Scripture?

5

New Patterns of Church Growth

Five Theological and Methodological Considerations

God Himself develops new ecclesiastical patterns. The first point to notice is that after Easter, the Gospel and the Mission, like the Lord Himself, took on a new form. The second point to notice is the very close association between the gift of the Holy Spirit and the Church's discharging of its Mission. The promise of the Spirit is specifically to enable the disciples to be witnesses. "But you shall receive power when the Holy Spirit has come upon you; and you shall be my witnesses in Jerusalem and in all Judea and Samaria and to the end of the earth." (Acts 1:8) In St. John, the bestowal of the Spirit and the bestowal of the great commission are linked together. "As the Father has sent me, even so I send you. And when he had said this, he breathed on them, and said to them, Receive the Holy Spirit." (John 20:21,22) The Church that came into being on the day of Pentecost was a witnessing Church. The Church of the first century of the Christian era was a witnessing, propagating Church and a prophetic one too.

There is an unchanging mission because God has revealed in Christ an eternal purpose. But God has sent forth His Church into this changing world. Tremendous changes are taking place in today's world. Especially in India, the current situation is very different from that which existed thirty years ago. It is very important for the Church to understand the times in which it exists in order to perform its mission effectively. Jesus has some very hard words to say about those who were unable to understand the times in which they lived. He says, "You know how to interpret the appearance of the sky, but you cannot interpret the signs of the times." (Matthew 16:3)

These general truths are nowhere more applicable than in regard to the evangelization of the Hindus in India. Here we may confidently expect the Holy Spirit to guide us into new forms. As the Gospel spreads to new strata of society, the Church will develop new structures.

Changes in India have made some Hindus Responsive

In Andhra Pradesh as well as in the whole of India, evangelizing Hindus has in the past not been very successful. However, in 1970, a most encouraging factor in Hindu evangelization is that the people are more responsive now than ever before. Present day India is very different from what it was before 1947. National independence and ever growing contact with other nations and peoples of the world have filled the minds of our people with new aspirations, and India is fast changing. When the new Andhra Pradesh came into being, it began feeling the freshness of a new life and attempting elaborate five-year plans to give more food, education, and health to its citizens. In the present situation in Andhra, there are tremendous opportunities for the Church to perform its primary task—evangelism based on the commission given by our Lord. The whole Church is to take the whole Gospel to the whole world.

The Chief Task and the Institutions

In a way, it is difficult to speak about today's task (singular) in missions, when hundreds of tasks lie before the Church. The internal administration itself can occupy the whole of life. Raising church budgets, helping Christians to grow in grace, and building churches are important; healing the sick, feeding the poor, taking care of education and all the rest of the social services are good. Yet, our great leaders never considered these anything but auxilliary services. The great task was to make Christ known.

> In mission today many tasks must be carried on together; yet the multiplicity of good activities must contribute to, and not crowd out, maximum reconciliation of men to God in the Church of Jesus Christ. God desires that men be saved in this sense that through faith they live in Christ and through obedience they are baptized in His name, and live as responsible members of His body. God, therefore, commands members of His household to go and make disciples of all nations. Fulfilling this command is the supreme purpose which should guide the entire mission, establish its priorities, and coordinate its activities. (McGavran 1970:51)

To be sure, McGavran insists and I agree that institutions like schools, colleges, and hospitals are a legitimate and useful part of the Church's mission.

D. T. Niles also makes this point very clear. He said:

> Christian institutions as an integral part of a Church structure is a phenomenon peculiar to the younger Churches in Asia, Africa, and Latin America. These schools, colleges, hospitals, agricultural institutes and the like were conceived as part of the Church's mission and had three objectives: the nurture of the Christian community, the service of the world, and the commendation of the Gospel. (1962:177)

But, everyone must recognize that most institutions which were once regarded as great channels of evangelistic enterprise have ceased to fulfil that aim long ago.

> That is why "a re-examination of the number, type, and character of institution in relation to the Church's total task" has become very necessary and we now need to ask "whether the resources claimed by some of these institutions should not be released for use in new enterprises closer to the local Church and more central to its missionary task." (Renewal and Advance 1963: 149)

Dr. John Mangum, an experienced mission policy planner of the Lutheran Church in America, insists that the institutions must contribute to God's mission to man. He says:

> The Church and all its organizations and institutions and agencies and commissions and boards and programmes and printed materials and audiovisuals and conventions and social statements and motions and minutes have no valid significance except as they contribute to God's mission to man. The two important elements in the situation are God and man. (1963:3)

A Dynamic Biblical Theory of Advance

What is currently referred to as the Church Growth Theory is but a gathering together and sharpening of concepts and methods which many missiologists have long advocated and used. Perhaps McGavran's greatest contribution to missions is in focusing these principles on the issues facing churches and missions today, and calling the Church's attention to the fact that in many parts of the world, they are providing solutions which result in sound Church growth. When, in this study, we speak of "Church Growth" we do not mean the spiritual or intellectual advance of existing members of the Church. Our study is concerned mainly with bringing my people—the Hindus—to the joy of becoming disciples of the Lord Jesus. The spread of the Church throughout the world must never be thought of in terms of Western Church expansion, nor in simply human terms.

"On the contrary," as Cullman (1961:46) says, "The Church itself is an eschatalogical phenomenon . . . constituted by the Holy Spirit." And as Dr. McGavran (1962:98) states:

> By "Church Growth" we mean a process of spiritual reproduction whereby new congregations are formed. The Church in New Testament times grew in this fashion. New congregations by the score sprang up where there had been none before. In our use of the term, a Church "grows" when it multiplies its membership and its congregations and then with ever increasing power takes into itself converts in a widening stream."

The Church, like the familiar sower who went forth to sow, invariably finds that not all the seeds of its message fall on soil conducive to growth. But some do, bringing forth abundant results. It the same way, all segments of society are not equally responsive to the Gospel. Some—among them many Hindus—are more responsive than others.

The Bible teaches that the Lord sends His disciples to "the harvest" and not merely to "the fields" (Matthew 9:37,38) Likewise, Christ commanded His disciples not to spend time and effort on the unresponsive (Matthew 10:14). This does not mean that the Church should pull out of resistant fields, but rather that the Church should first search out and harvest the ripe ones.

The time is ripe for the churches to multiply among Hindus in Andhra Pradesh. Harvest theology says that the Church must concentrate its efforts on cultivating the productive soil. Related to the principle of receptivity and ripeness of homogeneous units is that of "The People Movement," which relates to the process by which homogeneous units are most likely to become Christian.

A. L. Warnshuis, who was co-secretary of the International Missionary Council for many years, makes the following statement quoted by a well-known Lutheran Pastor J. C. Wold (1968:124)

> Briefly summarized, the wrong way to try and build up a Church in a non-Christian land is by the conversion of individuals extracted from dozens of groups. Such converts are promptly ostracized, separated from their relations and cut from their roots in the past of their own peoples. Such a Church is only a conglomeration of individuals—often held together only by the cement of foreign money. That kind of Church has no community and continues indefinitely dependent upon missionary aid.
>
> The better way is by recognition of the principle that the Church grows along racial lines in social strata. The right and natural growth of the Church is by the conversion of groups, where Christian forces help some group reconstruct its life, individual and corporate, around Jesus Christ.

A People Movement involves multi-individual decisions, meaning that many people participate each making up his own mind after debating with himself and others within his group. Each individual is saved not by going along with the crowd, but by his personal faith which led him to participate in the decision of the group.

Most of the Oceanic people have become Christians by group movements. A people movement that took place among the Papuan tribesmen in New Guinea is a classic example. The tribes as wholes burned their fetishes and became Christians under the leadership and direction of Missionary Christian Keyser of the Lutheran Church. The large Churches all around the world have all grown by group accessions of one variety or another.

The people movement, broadly defined, is too good a mode of growth and has too many valuable characteristics to let slip. Is there anything that we as human beings can do to bring about people movements? As Christians, we believe that all conversion (both individual and group) is the work of the Holy Spirit. "It is the Holy Spirit who calls, gathers, enlightens and sanctifies the whole Christian Church in the world." (Martin Luther, Small Catechism) Since the Holy Spirit obviously uses people movements to bring multitudes into redemptive relationship to Jesus Christ, the best thing we can do is to pray the Lord for such movements. We should ask Him to give us the power to discern the villages and people to whom the Spirit is leading us. The knowledge of anthropology and sociology can provide us with a true and exact knowledge of the culture of the people and thus help us discern the segments of society to which the Holy Spirit directs.

To give an example from the Scripture, in the case of the jailer, Paul converted the head of the household and the whole house became Christians. If he had converted one of the sons, the father might have been offended and nobody else might have accepted the Lord. So also in Andhra, the eldest members are so very important. They must be approached first and we must see that even if they themselves do not choose Christ, they do not provide a hindrance. If they do not become Christians, they can at least give their consent to other members.

The people movement principle says that it is far better to allow the faith to spread throughout the web relations of family, friends, and social strata before public commitment is asked of individuals. When individuals who are convinced of the Gospel and determined to become Christians form a "block" large enough to hold its own against the pressures of the remainder of the group, and exert a real evangelical influence among the still non-Christian element of their people, then they profess their faith.

Basically, the people movement principle says that a group is more likely to become Christian if the first "converts" to Christianity are not "pulled out" (often this means pushed out). socially dislocated from the group, and in effect set against their own people.

In Andhra, in a way, it is not so good separating some of the converts from their community and helping them to settle down in convert homes. Of course, much could be said on both sides, the situation was so terrible for the converts, that it almost became a necessity to save their lives. It could have been better had plans been made to send them back to their places when things got better. Instead, permanent arrangements were made for their lifetime settlement. This is part of the mission station approach. Along with schools and orphanages, quarters were built for the Hindu converts. In our Andhra Evangelical Lutheran Church, we have one such at Rajahmundry. The few individuals, from castes that accepted Christianity were forced out of their homes by fierce ostracism. Inevitably they came to live at the mission colony and it was here they were usually employed. This kind of mission station approach took shape out of the individualistic background. "To become a Christian" in the early days meant "to come out of one community and join another." With all its limitations, it was necessary in the beginning. For that era it was the best strategy. However now, it is high time to begin using thepeople movement approach.

The period of decision for a communal group may be long. It may spread over months or years as individuals, one by one, or in village or family discussions, come to the position where they can at least say that they are of one mind to follow Christ. Thus, this is a multi-individual decision.

> Once the decision for conversion has been made and the group has separated itself from the old context like the New Testament parable house swept of the evil spirit, it is vulnerable unless it can quickly achieve its new contextual entity. The new norms have to be fixed. The group entity has to be established. After a certain amount of instruction and training the transition is ritually effected and finally completed by means of an act of incorporation. (Tippett 1967: 6)

The People Movement Concept Applied to Hindu Ethnic Units

It may seem strange for me to be pleading in the Evangelical Lutheran Church for people movements because our great Church of 180,000 members came into being through a series of people movements to Christ. A series of caste-wise movements swept through our districts and taluks leaving Lutheran congregations in hundreds of villages. The people movement is well known to us. The previous generation called these movements by the opprobrious name "mass movements" and thus stigmatized them; but, whatever they were called, two of the ethnic units of our part of India turned responsive and were harvested. Men and women talked over becoming Christians together. When they were of one mind, they requested instruction and baptism. Our church records indicate clearly that on certain days perhaps a fourth, perhaps a half, and often an entire segment of the village were baptized on the same day. The ministers of our Church are mostly sons and grandsons of the first converts who flooded into the Church together, having made multi-individual decisions to accept the Lord Jesus Christ as their Saviour.

Yet my pleading is not out of place. For though the Harijans came to Christ group by group and family by family without leaving their kinfolk, without joining another social unit, and without going to worship in a different part of the village, today considerable sentiment exists which apparently requires the Kammas and Reddys, Lambadis and Kapus to become Christians one by one, to leave their kinfolk, to become worshipping members of another social unit, and not to build churches in their own sections of the villages. What I am really saying therefore, is this: Just as God led the Harijans between 1870 and 1940 to become Christians in a long people movement, so He is leading other ethnic groups today and will lead still others tomorrow.

These should not be asked to become Christians in the new patterns which the Lutheran missionaries established and the Harijans found convenient, The older people movement within homogeneous units pattern which is more indigenous, more suited to the land-owning segments of the population—should not only be allowed, but should be encouraged.

It is worthy of note that to date the only pattern allowed by the Harijan Churches to the middle castes is to join the congregations of those ethnic units which from time immemorial have been considered "outcaste." Because of this, only a very few have become Christians. These have turned to Christ one by one against the social current. A woman here without her husband, a son there without his father, a daughter without the rest of her family. It is a great testimony to the power of Christ and the good will which sometimes develops between the various castes in our Indian villages that here and there a dozen or so individuals from the middle castes in a given village have become Christians and have gone to the existing church to worship and commune; but it is also a great testimony to the barriers which divide the castes that these few Christians have not as a rule been able to win their families, their husbands, their caste-fellows, their brothers, and their children to Christ. Why should a church which arose through the people movement impose on new converts the "one-by-one-out-of-a-caste" mode of church growth?

New to this generation though historically older patterns of church growth are needed. Let me mention only a few. I am writing this in Pasadena, California. Here are many Lutheran churches in the same city. There is nothing in the Bible which says that we must have only one congregation per village. Indeed, the pattern of the synagogue was that any twelve Jews provided they were above the age of twelve and were males, could start a new synagogue. Why not gladly allow as many congregations as the Christians desire in each of the villages of our districts in Andhra? Back in 1900, we Indians would have fiercely resented having to go to the European sections of Guntur or Madras to worship. We wanted churches in our own neighbourhoods. We wanted churches full of our kind of people. Why, in some villages to this day, the Mala community has its Lutheran church and the Madiga community its own. It is no sin for a denomination to have several churches in one village community—or if there is, America is full of very sinful denominations!

Communication Theory Urges Recognition of Social Strata

In Andhra Pradesh, out of 35,983,447 persons, 29,708,939 (1961 Census of India) live in thousands of villages, and each village and especially each caste group in each village composes a "Face-to-Face Society." Nida describes four basic principles in communicating effectively in such a society which applies to these thousands of villages.

> (1) Effective communication must be based upon personal friendship; (2) The initial approach should be to those who can effectively pass on communication within their family grouping; (3) Time must be allowed for the internal diffusion of new ideas; and (4) The challenge for any change of belief or action must be addressed to the persons or groups, socially capable of making such decisions. (1960:110)

Nida gives the example of John Ritchie, an outstanding missionary in Peru. He always went to the home of the villager who had invited him. His host might not be a Christian but must be interested in the Good News, After establishing friendship in one village, it was not difficult for him to get invitations from other villages. Because of the family relationships, the word passes on to many areas. Communication works exactly in the same way in Andhra.

Nida summarizes certain observations concerning the response to the Gospel in "Face-to-Face Societies" as follows:

> (1) The response to the preaching of the Good News may at times reflect a social situation, even more

> than a religious conviction. (2) Opposition to the communication of the Christian message may be in many instances more social than religious. (3) Changes in social structure may alter the religious view of behaviour. (4) Effective communication follows the patterns of social structure. (5) A relevant witness will incorporate valid indigenous social structures. (1960: 132,133)

It is an established fact that effective communication within any social context must follow the social structure. An effective Church always incorporates into its structure the valid indigenous forms of social organizations.

Indigenous Church Principles Demand Freedom of Each People to Follow Its Own Culture

We have ample evidence to show that Hindus in Andhra are more responsive to the Gospel than ever. In my questionnaires 1 and 2, for the question, "Are Hindus responsive to the Gospel"? the response was an emphatic "Yes" from all; but church growth from among Hindus is nevertheless very little. This situation indicates the urgent need for a revised approach. Whatever methods we might use, they must work with the culture (and sub-culture) not against it.

The Church must come to grips with the undertaking of the situation in which it can present the Gospel of redemption meaningfully in this new Andhra of ours. As in other parts of the world, rapid social changes are taking place in Andhra. Secularism is rapidly spreading. There is a continual struggle for freedom from the traditional patterns of life. There is a steady quest for human dignity and betterment of life. Our mission and message have to be related to this new upsurge for a fuller life. Our Lord has said "I have come that they may have life and have it abundantly." (John 10: 10b)

Indigenous churches "spring up in the soil from the very first seeds planted" said Allen. They create their own structures and polity which evolve naturally from the patterns already common to the local culture and society. The indigenous Church---free to follow its own culture---among the middle classes will necessarily be different from the existing congregations formed so largely from the landless. "For any religious conversion to be permanent, its new structure should both meet the needs of the converts and operate in meaningful forms. It is thus that new indigenous religion is born." (Tippett 1967:6)

Truly indigenous churches from amongst the Hindus will pay more attention to the family than existing churches do. Among Hindus, the family is the social unit that must be taken into consideration. It might be the only social institution through which the Gospel can spread and be established. The Jews, through suffering contempt and persecution of various societies throughout their long history have found in their home life privacy, independence, self respect, and meaning which gave them strength to maintain their way of life and faith. So can those Hindus who become disciples of Christ.

So in Andhra one must make the best possible use of this greatest resource for church growth. A close examination of the community is sufficient to convince one that family and village units can be approached and be baptized like the jailer at Philippi (Acts 17:34) who was baptized together with "all who were in his house."

It is not enough to recognize that the family is the social unit that we can work through, it is all the more important to know what constitutes a family. The biological relationships differ from one society to another. In Andhra, more among the middle classes than among the Harijans, the family pattern is slowly changing. We still have the joint family system. (Appendix E) In order to find out how we can disciple families and groups of families, we must relate it learn from it.

Fitting Worship to the Converts

While considering indigenous churches among Hindus, prior importance must be given to the worship. Pickett, in his survey of Indian churches, found out that the churches which are worshipping daily and participating regularly in the Lord's Supper are the living ones. Converts must be provided with the proper kind of worship.

The existing Church has adopted mostly the Western pattern of worship. In many churches, especially in towns, people sit on benches to worship. Hindus do not feel at home doing it this way. In many of their temples and even in their houses, the proper way to worship is to sit on the floor and at times, prostrate one oneself before the gods and goddesses. When they are at any holy river or worshipping the sun, they stand, fold their hands, and pay homage to their gods.

Our Ashramites always enjoy kneeling down in prayer. When we go to "Christ Church" in Luthergiri (Rajahmundry) they go clear to the front, prostrate themselves and say their prayers. One convert, Ramayamma, who attends "Christ Church," sits on the floor even though we all sit on the benches and happily worships the Lord.

The service should be kept to the standard of Indian people, leaving room for more participation by the members. Music must be indigenous and the native musical instruments should be used. It is also good to observe silence at certain points during the service.

These and many other changes can be introduced in our Lutheran worship so that the visitors and converts from the Hindu community might feel at home and have the benefit of the Christian worship of God. Above all, "A truly indigenous worship will be the natural offering of a church that knows itself to be God's people in India, a church alive to its mission of claiming India for Christ." (Grant 1959:74)

New Patterns of Church Growth Involve New Ways of Evangelism

I make no apology for borrowing rather freely from A. G. Hogg, a noted professor in Madras Christian College in India, an eminent theologian. His book on The Christian Message to the Hindu is worth translating into many Indian languages. In the following pages, while the thoughts expressed are my own, I have lit my candle at his fire.

I am convinced that the Holy Spirit is preparing many Hindus in Andhra for the acceptance of the Gospel. However, there is urgent need to use new and suitable methods to evangelize these receptive populations.

First of all, it must be borne in mind that for valid reasons the approach to orthodox Hindus needs to be different than that to Harijans. As we have seen under social structures, as well as in the case studies, the Harijans have always been kept separate. Their religious life was confined to their small section of the residential area. They did not even have the opportunity to worship in the common temple until the recent Temple Entry Act was passed. Before the missions came, education among them was very slight indeed. They were in need of physical, mental, and spiritual redemption.

Hogg makes a clear distinction between the religions of the Harijans and Hindus. Most of the beliefs of the Harijan community, he thinks, have an animistic base.

But the section of the population that we propose to evangelize is really impregnated with the ideas and aspirations of India's characteristic religious heritage. They are for the most part extremely religious people. You will find every village with at least one temple and, in many cases, there is a temple on almost every street corner. There is an idol or shrine in nearly every home. However small the house may be, the householder sets apart a room or corner for the gods and goddesses. "Religion dominates their life from the cradle to the grave. Almost everything the Indian does has some religious significance attached to it." (Seamands 1964:115)

Hindus take pride in their religion. They talk about religion anywhere—in the house as well as in the public places like shops, trains, or busses. Hindus observe religious practices with great care. Both men and women take time to have their sacred baths and to begin the day with worship. They are not ashamed to practise their religion. Often you see a Hindu stop on the street to bow and worship at some wayside shrine. There is no end to their fastings and pilgrimages. Even the most intelligent and educated people participate in all kinds of religious activities.

The guru plays a very important part in the life of a Hindu as I know very well since my uncle is a guru. There are different kinds of gurus. It is almost an essential thing for a religious person to become a disciple of some guru and for the most part they will be under the influence of that guru who has at least some knowledge of the religion. Sometimes Christians give the Gospel to an ordinary Hindu and he discusses it with his guru and into higher circles.

Unless the approach is on the guru's level, it has very little chance of winning Hindus for Christ. In all this, my emphasis is that our approach needs to be very different from that to the Harijans which has been used for the last hundred years. If anybody believes that we can disciple these Hindu people in the same way that we did the Harijans, he is much mistaken (except for the probability that people movements will result if the proper approach is employed).

Is it not important to give the fullest recognition to the very different people to whom we now address ourselves? Is diversity in approach unscriptural? Did not Paul accommodate himself to his audience? He himself spoke of his becoming all things to all men that he might by all means save some. It is worth noting I Corinthians 9:19-21.

> For though I am no man's slave, yet I have made myself everyone's slave, that I might win more men to Christ. To the Jews I was a Jew that I might win the Jews. To those who were under the law I put myself in the position of being under the law (although in fact I stand free of it), that I might win those who are under the law. To those who had no law I myself became like a man without the law (even though in fact I cannot be a lawless man for I am bound by the law of Christ), so that I might win men who have no law. (Phillips Translation)

However, the Christian message to the Hindu must never be merely a slightly Christian version of Hinduism but it should give to the authentic Christian faith a truly Indian form of expression. In the modes of presentation adopted, there must always be a challenging relevancy.

> There must be challenge for it is a unique Gospel that the Church is commissioned by its Lord to declare. But if the challenge is to be made effectively it must be concentrated at key positions and not dissipated by being spread over every point where Christian and Hindu ways of thought diverge. (Hogg 1947:11)

The message needs not only to be challengingly conceived, but relevantly expressed. It must meet the hearer at some point where he is conscious, or can be made conscious, of a spiritual need.

The most important of all the Hindu doctrines is "Transmigration." Unless we engage their thinking along this line, we do not succeed in relating the Good News to their utmost need. In the following passage, Dr. Hogg discusses the need to speak to the conviction of the Hindu about transmigration. His succeeding argument (seven pages of chapter I) illustrates the complexity of the situation and emphasizes that an evangelistic approach directed exactly to the believing Hindu must be used.

> Traditionally rooted in the mind of the orthodox Hindu is the conviction that, unless a way of salvation can be found, he is condemned to an endless process of reincarnation—an indefinitely continuing chain of lives, all of them unsatisfying and cursed with the falsity of illusion. It is from this dreary prospect that the orthodox Hindu seeks to be rescued. That is what he understands by salvation. It would be useless for you to begin your preaching by asserting that he stands in no such danger, and that the whole idea of an endless chain of lives is a myth. For he would not believe you, and the assertion would only provoke a mood of controversy that is fatal to the purpose of the preacher. But if, on the other hand, you simply ignore the entire subject and proclaim the Gospel in the manner you would follow in your homeland, will not your Hindu listeners feel that you have no message for them, since your thought seems never to have come to terms with that ultimate moral necessity which haunts their consciousness—the ultimate moral necessity whereby the wages of action is reincarnation? (Hogg 1947:21)

Whatever might be the approach, the ultimate answer is to be found only in the revealed Word. We do well by introducing the Hindus to the Scriptures. The living Word certainly speaks to people and transforms their lives. Solutions for problems like rebirth which we have discussed will certainly be found. Once the Bible is accepted as God's Word a most intelligent and well-informed person like Narayan Vaman Tilak, the famous Marathi poet, could not escape the life binding power of the Word. When a New Testament was given to Tilak by a travelling companion, he disliked it at first sight, but promised to read it for the sake of gratifying the good man who gave it to him; but did not keep his promise.

Months later, for want of any other book, he decided to keep his promise. He thought that he could follow his usual practice of reading the book through from beginning to end, marking the passages worthy of more thought. But he had an entirely different experience with this particular book which he expresses in the following way.

> It became impossible to leave these jewel-like sentences, so filled with love, mercy and truth. The most difficult questions of Hindu philosophy found their answer in these three chapters of Saint Matthew. I was most astonished to see problems like that of rebirth fully resolved, and filled with desire for more knowledge of Christ. I read eagerly on to the end. A Christian police superintendent gave me a little book and bundles of tracts. Among them I found a book called "The Character of Jesus." After reading it my hunger for a knowledge of the life of Christ grew. (Tilak 1956:37)

This has been the experience of many converts in India. The well known Sadhu Singh burnt the first Bible given to him but when he came back to the Word of God, he found Christ. One day a European professor of comparative religions---an agnostic---interviewed Sadhu Singh with the evident intention of showing him his mistake in renouncing another faith for Christ.

> He asked, "What have you found in Christianity that you did not have in your old religion"? The Sadhu answered, "I have Christ." "Yes, I know," the professor replied somewhat impatiently, "but what particular principles or doctrine have you found that you did not have before"? Sundar Singh replied, "The particular thing that I have found is Christ." Try as the professor might, he could not budge him from that position. He went away discomforted but thoughtful.

> The Sadhu was right. The religions of the world have fine things in them, but they lack Christ. (Seamands 1964:65-66)

All our attempts should focus on presenting Christ to the Hindus. This is their real lack. There are fine things in their culture and thought. Their Scriptures have profound doctrines. But they have no Christ. And lacking Him, their life lacks its supreme necessity.

The doctrine of karma is another big thing in Hinduism that has to be taken into account in our approach. The concept of transmigration which we discussed is founded on karma. The term "karma" means simply action or deed. What we have to understand is the employment of this word in such sentences as: "this misfortune of mine is just my karma"? I have no intention of discussing this topic at length, but I would like to mention it for further study. Basing on this doctrine, a typical Hindu's declaration is: "There is no problem, for there is no undeserved suffering." The truly Christian declaration is: "There is no problem, for it is right that there should be undeserved suffering." (Hogg 1947: 79) Therefore, we must go into the matter and see whether we can declare the Gospel in a manner that is completely relevant to Hindu thought about karma. Hogg states the matter very clearly:

> "Be sure," said Moses, "your sin will find you out." On the face of it the karma—transmigration concept would seem to be an acceptance of that Mosaic proverb, but in real fact it is its negation. If my sin is really to find me out, I must perceive that it is my sin and how horribly sinful it is. But according to the karma transmigration concept the sin that is finding me out is always a sin of the nature of which I have no knowledge because it was committed by me in an unnumbered previous incarnation. Such an experience is no moral searching of the conscience. Only as I find out my sin's sinfulness can I be morally found out by my sin. And the supremely adequate way of being found out by my individual sin is when I discover that in God's judgment it can be morally dealt with in no lesser way than by His own incarnation unto death. (Hogg 1947:87)

Modern Methods of Communication

While we are on the important topic of "new ways of evangelism," let us consider some of the modern methods to communicate the Gospel to the large segments of the Hindu population, each of which has very different standards of life.

There is a great need to re-examine not only the contents but also the form of proclamation of the Gospel. It is true there are still many illiterates even among caste people, but H. R. Weber is right in saying

> It is fundamentally wrong to treat illiterates as children and merely to tell them Bible stories. They are much better equipped than many Western intellectuals to see the whole and complete redemptive history— creation and eschatology, Christ the centre of redemption, and linked with this centre the history of Israel and of the mission. (1957:44)

They must be treated like adults. Communication, which begins with a confrontation of one faith by another, must rest on a two-way traffic of witnesses. We can only confront mythological thinking with redemptive history, if our proclamation comprises the whole of the Bible and the message of the Old and the New Testaments. So it is wrong to tell the converts only the things from the New Testament, as is frequently done. It is also not so good to translate only the New Testament, or portions of it, as is the general practice in many countries.

As we know, this is the age of "population explosions." To reach all the large population of Hindus is a tremendous task. We need to reach more people with the Gospel in less time and to preach effectively. Research has shown that people remember only 10 per cent of what they hear and about 50 per cent of what they see, so visual aids can be of great help to drive home the Gospel message.

All efforts should be made to confront the educated Hindus with the printed word. Fortunately, we have more literates now to help our cause. In Andhra, the per cent of literacy was 13.1 per cent in 1951. It lifted to 21.2 per cent by 1961. Christians will be wise to use the current opportunity.

In Andhra as well as in the whole of India, Christianity became the religion of the lowest social classes. In a way, we are glad it happened that way, otherwise the caste communities might have accepted Christ first and it would have been more difficult for Harijans to find their way to Christianity because of the social oppression. On the other hand, Christianity stayed with Harijans instead of spreading to the other communities. This is a bad sign.

Most of the effort and money of missions and Church is put into perfecting the existing Church. Jesus said, "Disciple all the nations." Very little attention is paid to this aspect of the work. J. T. Seamands, in his book The Supreme Task of the Church, gives the following illustration which very well explains the situation in Andhra. Jesus said, "The field is the world." What would you think of a farmer who kept on working one little corner of his field year after year, while he let the rest of the land go untilled and unsown! I am sure we would say he was foolish. Then what about the Church that keeps on ministering to the same small segment of the population year after year, but does nothing to take the Good News to those all around who have never heard. Especially when people want the Gospel and even ask for it it is sinful not to take the task of communicating the Good News seriously.

Urban Church Planting

The most neglected area in which to multiply churches is the urban. I include cities, towns, and the fast growing industrial centres under this category. The little discipling that has been done among Hindus has mostly been concentrated in villages. Of course, this is important. The potentialities of the great rural Church are very great. With all the handicaps of their poverty and illiteracy, the village people have a potentiality far beyond the estimation of some city dwellers who are educated. But this does not exempt or free us from our responsibilities to 6,274,508 people who live in the 223 towns and cities of Andhra Pradesh (Census of India 1961:37, supplies the data).

Industrial Evangelism

In recent years, more and more people are migrating to city and town areas. Industrial belts are suddenly springing up in and around Hyderbad, Rajahmundry, Visakhapatnam, and other cities. Industrialization has brought about changes in the economy, and also in India's social and cultural life.

In this changing situation, there are great opportunities to multiply churches in most industrial belts. We can proclaim Christ and encourage industrial men to become Christians right where they are in the place of their work. It is gratifying to note that under the auspices of the National Christian Council of India, an international team of industrial missionaries spent six months visiting churches in the principal industrial centres of the country with the purpose of helping the churches to see their responsibility for the very large number of non-Christians who live there.

Under the five-year plans, more and more industries are coming into existence. Right where I live in Rajahmundry, three big industries have been established---paper mills, quaries, and tobacco factories. Thousands work in them and listen attentively to the Gospel. There are good possibilities of discipling them. Our Bible Training School works mainly with the women and children in quaries. Whenever we go there, they receive us with gladness and learn with great enthusiasm what we teach. They migrate from different areas of Andhra; they come from simple village life to the complex and crowded urban centres, Moreover, they leave behind their relatives and familiar neighbours and also their favourite idols. When they are just looking for new contacts and trying to feel their way, we can certainly help them with our friendship and introduce them to the Gospel. Some of them have been baptized in "Christ Church," the Lutheran Church in which I worship. It is a joy to see them on Sunday morning in church service, foregoing even their income for the day. Once they decide to be Christians, they give up all pagan practices, learn all we can teach them about Christ, and insist that we baptize them. We should certainly do more work among them and plant a number of churches in their neighbourhood.

Evangelism in Towns and Cities

In fairness, it must be said that the missions have planted some churches in urban areas. Most of the mission stations are located in prominent towns and cities. The majority of the missionaries live in urban centres. Of course, almost all the institutions like secondary schools and colleges and hospitals are established in urban centres. But the problem is that churches are not multiplying in cities in spite of all the "mission work" going on there.

The general feeling is that the town folk are not responsive. This does not sound right. The Early Church grew in the great cities like Jerusalem, Antioch, and Alexandria. Paul set a good example in starting churches in the strategic areas. As a matter of fact, in towns with all the modern conveyance facilities and audio-visual equipment, we have much more chance to communicate the Gospel. We also have theologically trained personnel. Yet not much fruit is shown. Perhaps the trouble is that we do not try to plant many new congregations.

There is an urgent need for research. First of all, the town folk should not be treated as one big homogeneous unit, because in fact they are composed of many language groups, occupations, castes and other units of society. We should discover which units are the most receptive. This kind of investigation will enable us to devise an intelligent approach of each unit.

Training Urban Church Planters

Besides other things, the greatest need seems to be trained leaders for the planting of churches. Unfortunately, the defect lies right in the training itself. Seminaries are producing theologians and preachers not church planters. In order to train church planters, the theological school itself must act as a church planting institution. For example, Andhra Christian Theological College at Rajahmundry can and should be planting congregations in different parts of the town. At present, they participate in evangelism programmes once a week, and help in the parishes, but they can easily concentrate on planting new churches. This would provide the proper training for the students to carry on the same type of important task in all their later life.

Urban church planting is an important issue in the modern age. Ways of effective church establishment have to be found out. As a guide for our work among Hindus in Andhra, I would like to mention six keys to church growth in cities suggested by Dr. McGavran.

1. Emphasis on House Churches. People are used to community life. The idea of house churches fits well into their pattern of life. Some of the middle-class people have big enough houses to use as places of worship. Many of them would be willing to lend their homes for this type of sacred task. Indeed, this is deeply satisfying to the Indian mind. There is no difficulty in getting people together in a house church in Andhra. If the beginning is made by way of a house church, soon Christians will normally end up with a good church building. Many of them, while Hindus, freely contribute to the erection of Hindu temples. I am sure those who become Christians will gladly contribute to the erection of Christian churches.

2. Unpaid Lay Leaders. Hundreds of leaders are needed if the work is to be carried on successfully. Effort should, therefore, be made to find out the natural leaders among all groups of converts. These will usually be glad to give time for the work of the church including the many things which are to be done for and with the believers. Since Christians are usually scattered across cities, the more unpaid lay leaders we have the better. They can multiply house churches in the various parts of the towns and cities.

As a rule, unpaid workers are respected and listened to. We have many men and women with different talents who earn their livelihood either by manual labour or business. Some of them are well-to-do people deriving income from property inherited from their ancestors. They can afford to give free service in the church. Such unpaid natural leaders should be carefully trained.

3. Recognize Resistant Homogeneous Units. Certain sections of our Andhra towns are resistant to the Gospel. I know of some places in Rajahmundry, Guntur, and Hyderabad

whose residents belong exclusively to Brahmin castes and Islam. They are very slow, indeed, to respond to the Gospel. It would be an unfortunate experience to evangelize such segments first and thus get discouraged and stop witnessing.

4. Focus on the Responsive. It must be recognized that certain areas of the city are more receptive than others. For some reason or other, even in the towns many middle-class people are readily accepting the Good News. We must not only evangelize such people, but must plant churches right in their midst. Only then will the Gospel spread like fire over the whole section in which such people live.

5. Surmount the Property Barrier. The house church pattern is excellent to begin with; but for all practical reasons, sooner or later a separate church should be built. To secure land in the crowded towns in Andhra is rather difficult, but if enough people get interested in the Gospel, they will surely find a convenient spot to build at least a temporary structure. Later, this can be developed into a permanent building. Converts from caste background have had the experience of contributing generously to the Hindu temples so they can be counted on to build a church for worship which they value highly.

6. Communicate Intense Belief. The prime ingredient in the capture of the great cities of the ancient world was fervent faith. This is evident in the New Testament and was the experience of all planters of the Early Church. The Revelation of John is convincing evidence of the climate of faith in that city-conquering church.

> Do not fear what you are about to suffer. Behold, the devil is about to throw some of you into prison, that you may be tested, and for ten days you will have tribulation.
>
> Be faithful to death and I will give you the crown of life.... He who conquers shall not be hurt by the second death.... (Revelation 2:10,11)
>
> After this behold a great multitude which no man could number, from every nation, from all tribes, and peoples, and tongues, standing before the throne and before the lamb....and one of the elders said .... "These are those who have come out of the great tribulation." (Revelation 7:9)

No human power can spread Christianity throughout the urban areas. It is only made possible by the work of the Holy Spirit.

Above all, research in the whole matter of urban evangelization is urgent. We do not really know what makes the churches grow in cities. An analysis of the whole situation will help find our way to proceed in the right direction. I wish the concerned church bodies would make an effort to carry on research in urban church multiplication. This will greatly benefit evangelization of Andhra's cities.

6

New Patterns of Leadership

The success of any programme depends on its personnel. To disciple the great number of Hindus in Andhra Pradesh, we certainly need hundreds and thousands of men and women. Before I could draw up plans for developing such, I thought it would be very helpful to survey the evangelistic programme of Protestant and Roman Catholic Churches in Andhra.

Church Leaders on the Effectiveness of Pastors and Workers from Caste Background

When writing this thesis, I sent out a questionnaire (Appendix A) to eleven Churches, ten Protestant and one Roman Catholic.*

All of them said that Hindus are "very responsive to the Gospel." They indicated that training converts to work among

* I am grateful to the following five church officials who kindly answered the questionnaire: The Rt. Rev. P. Solomon, Bishop of the Dornakal Diocese and the Moderator of the Church of South India; Fr. P. Innaiah, Bishop's secretary of the Roman Catholic Church; Mr. K. D. Benjamin, treasurer, South Andhra Lutheran Church; Mr. G. German, Godavary Delta Mission; and the Rev. S. W. Schmitthenner, president of the Andhra Evangelical Lutheran Church.

their own people is very useful. Bishop Solomon, answering question number nine (Do you see any advantage of training and using such personnel?), wrote "Yes, there is definitely." He also added, "I have seen preachers and pastors working enthusiastically among the people of their own background, for example Malas among Malas and those of Madiga origin pastors among Madigas, etc. Emotionally and culturally, it is encouraging."

For the same question, Fr. P. Innaiah answered, "Very useful." He described the method that the Catholic Church is practising.

> In the attempts we make to approach the caste people, particularly those castes with a social status like Reddys, Kammas, Salees, Thogatas, and Balijas, it is highly necessary that a priest resides among the people. We are approaching and planning out the method of presentation.

(Fr. P. Innaiah: Answer to question number eleven)

Mr. G. German said:

> We have a number of men and women of Hindu background who are full time workers....We have two couples stationed in the Papikondalu who have had the joy of baptizing about fifty Koyyas in that area.

The Rev. S. W. Schmitthenner, in his case study, explained at length how the convert women have been highly successful in discipling their friends and relatives. He also made the following statement:

> Out of 200 pastors, we have 6 who are from the Sudhras or Brahmin castes who are all young men, most of whom have been picked in recent years by their synod ministeriums... to have these men in the ministry.

Mr. K. D. Benjamin also said "yes" to the ninth question. These answers, from the responsible and experienced officers of the different churches, make it clear that for communicating the Gospel a leader from a caste background fits in better with a caste group. Vidyarthi makes the following statement regarding leadership:

> Man is a social being and a social group requires guidance. Guidance is to be given by someone to whose

directions and dictations every one submits. Such a person is known as a leader. (1967:67)

New Structures Demand New Patterns of Leadership

The Ministry of the Church in the New Testament. The methods we are going to study are not really new. They are rather those of the apostolic ministry described in the New Testament. There were two classes of apostles. The "apostles of Christ" who received their commission (apostleship) from the Risen Lord directly and the "apostles of the Church" (Acts 13:3, 14:14; II Corinthians 8:23; Philemon 2:25) commisioned by some local church. The continuing ministry of the Church is the apostolic ministry.

In the priestly ministry, "bishop" and "presbyter" are two words for the same function. The serving ministry finds Jesus, the apostles, and the humblest believers all given the title of "servant." It especially signifies service to others. Following the example of the Son of Man (Mark 10:45), every one has a service, a ministry in the Body of Christ.

What then, is the normative pattern of church life and ministry in the New Testament. W. D. Davies suggests a three-fold criteria:

> First, the Church was subject to order, deriving much of its form from the synagogue. Second, variety was the time of the day. There was no single order of service, no stereotyped fixed form. Thirdly, there was a clear sense of unity. Diverse in its external expression, the spirit is nevertheless creative of unity, a unity, we emphasize, which is not dependent on a unity of outward form nor destroyed by varieties of outward form, but which transcends all merely organizational differences.... This, then, is the third make of the New Testament Church: unity of the faith and universalism in appeal are not broken by diversity in organization. (1962:222)

Another important thing that we should study is the form of the Church. Maybe to our great surprise we find,

> The order of the Church was an evolving order, at

first including monarchic, oligarchic, and democrtic under the same roof, though gradually developing monepiscopacy of the second century (See Green: 1964, 42-50). Streeter has made this point forcefully. Lastly, the Church in the New Testament is the society called into being by the direct act of God in Christ. It is His Church; it is the community subject to his sovereignty, ministering for the Master to a wandering and rebelling world. Thus one finds that the form of the New Testament Church---monarchy, oligarchy, democracy---is not the vital thing. For the organization is not to be likened to the body, but to the clothes that cover the body. The structure of the Church is not something which, if altered will cause death, but is like clothes, some of which fit a situation and some of which do not. It is the ministry of the Church which is the lifeblood. No participation in the service of apostleship, priesthood of believers, and humble service . . . these are the significant features in the ministry of the New Testament. Then the Church today should not look primarily for men who can bear the same names as those recorded in the New Testament, but for men who perform the same ministries: apostleship, preaching, teaching oversight and God-given service, fitted to the cultural setting. (Wolf, term paper, n/d.:5,6)

The Indigenous Leadership

Every society has its own system of leadership. As the society becomes Christian, the Church should pattern its organization upon that of the society. Since we are dealing with Andhra Pradesh and its Christian leadership, it is important for us to remember Andhra's social structure and religious patterns as described in chapter one: Hinduism accepts and respects religious leaders. Gurus play a very important part in day-to-day life. They are all natural leaders and self-made men and women.

An indigenous leader has decisive advantages over any non-indigenous leader (indigenous to that ethnic unit). He knows the customs and traditions of the group. By the use of the vernacular and of customary manners and expressions, he can communicate well with his own people. He can share common interest and sentiment with members of the group. He can avoid culture shock in introducing change to his group. Every society has its own culture and every person is subject to the culture of the society of which he is a part.

To his own society, the indigenous leader can communicate the supracultural Gospel without mixing it with another culture and thus confusing his people.

This is true of subcultures also. For example, in Andhra, we have different homogeneous groups like Hindus and Harijans. The best leadership pattern can be attained when each group has its own leaders. For discipling the multicultural population of Andhra, the differences between subcultural groups need to be taken seriously.

> God's desire to reach man where he is, however, extends even beyond the adaptations required by culture. Ultimately, in fact, God adapts his approach to meet each individual where he is. But in between the cultural level and the individual level are a variety of levels which may be termed "subcultural."
> (Kraft, unpublished material)

The effectiveness of leadership can be evaluated in terms of its accomplishments toward a prescribed goal or goals.

> The leadership which facilitates communication with the group, makes for better morale, increases members' satisfaction, promotes greater productivity, and helps the group to move toward its goals without causing much friction among the group members, is usually understood as effective leadership. This suggests the need for special skills, personality resources, and knowledge of the dynamics of members of the group contributes to the effectiveness in leadership.
> (Vidyarthi 1967:63)

Luzbetak, the well-known anthropologist, puts great emphasis on indigenous leadership. He says that the deep effect of enculturation on the individual makes indigeniety important for developing native leadership in young Churches. He draws our attention to the official policy of the Church of

Rome which has been to choose leaders from among the local people. As recorded in Scripture (Titus 1:5), St. Paul ordered Titus to ordain native Cretans for the Cretan Church.

Luzbetak says that the Church of Rome commands the development of native leadership. Pius XI said:

> We are convinced that, unless you provide to the very best of your ability for native priests, your apostolate will remain crippled and the establishment of a fully-organized church in your territories will encounter still further delay . . . you should not conclude that the role of the local clergy is merely to help the foreign missionaries in lesser matters or in some minor fashion to supplement their work (Rerum Ecclesiae: 22,24). (Luzbetak 1970:104)

The answers to the questionnaires, the New Testament pattern, and the anthropological approach all draw our attention to the great need for indigenous leadership. In Andhra, this has been talked about only in contrast to leaders from the West, i.e. missionaries. It is becoming clear, however, that subcultures are to be treated as distinct homogeneous units. We are to train indigenous leaders from each unit for further church planting in that unit.

The Types and the Levels of Leaders

For the total ministry of the Church which includes evangelism and discipling, Andhra needs five types of leaders at different levels.

(1) The Specialists. Industrial belts are suddenly springing up in and around the cities like Rajahmundry and Visakhapatnam. Industrialization has brought about changes not only in the economy, but also making an impact on its social life. In this changing situation, there may be many opportunities to disciple the masses in these centres. We also have much need for chaplains in the hospitals and among students. Furthermore there is a need for

(2) Urban Church Pastors.

(3) Rural Church Pastors.

(4) Leaders for Christian Education.

(5) Church Planters among Hindus.

A whole book could be written on the first four kinds of leaders. However, I would like now to deal in detail with the fifth kind of leaders we need in Andhra—Church Planters among Hindus.

At the outset, we need to alter our concept of the ministry which now centres in clerical control.

> As Paton has pointed out: 'The idea of the professional clergyman which has been taken for granted in almost all our churches is required neither by Scripture nor by tradition.' (1965:11)

Such a concept, Paton says, has contributed immeasurably to the sterility of the Church in China (1953: Hayward, 1955).

And yet, as a World Council of Churches' study document points out,

> 'When St. Paul and his colleagues first preached the Gospel in Asia Minor, they entrusted to their first converts the responsibility for ministering in the congregations.... The new congregations had from the beginning the fulness of life in Christ ministered to them in word and sacrament. Modern missions have been unable to follow this pattern because they were dominated by a conception of the ministry as a paid professional class of men having academic and cultural qualifications required for this ministry in the countries from which the missionaries had come (1963: Vol. 52, 49-50). (Swanson 1968:371)

The belief and the practice of the past that every church must have a paid pastor or evangelist, and the insistence that it must also have a building, stand in the way of developing natural leaders. These ideas prevent the expansion of the Gospel by preventing the multiplication of churches. We must consider adopting a New Testament concept of ministry. We must also bear in mind the social background of the Hindu communities we are dealing with. Because of the variations in culture, leadership should be flexible and varied. Its pattern may best be somewhat parallel to the culture pattern of the section of society being discipled.

For the leader, two of the most important criteria are as follows. First, he must be one of the people, in social contact with those he serves, share their problems, and understand their needs. Second, he must be trained in Biblical and churchly learning and in the practice of the Christian life.

Theological Education

My use of the term "theological education" includes Bible institutes, Bible schools, and seminaries.

In an evaluation of present theological education in Andhra, the research I carried out included a brief survey. According to the questionnaire I sent to the theological institutes, the following kinds of workers are being trained. Andhra Christian Theological College prepares pastors for the churches in Andhra, the Licentiate of Theology. Ramapatnam Theological Seminary trains pastors and grants graduates the degrees of Bachelor of Divinity and Certificate in Theology. The Lutheran Bible Training Institute trained fifteen candidates for the year 1969-70 for entrance into the Licentiate of Theology course. The Retreat Training Centre at Masulipatnam trains men and women in short courses (ten to twenty days) for voluntary service.

But, none of the men's theological institutions in Andhra trains workers specifically to disciple Hindus or to multiply churches among them.

I also sent two questionnaires to two institutions in the province of Madras: The Hindustan Bible Institute and Gurukal Theological College. I received a reply from the Hindustan Bible Institute only. This institution trains evangelists, pastors, Sunday school workers, and missionaries. Dr. N. Paul V. Gupta, the director of the above institution adds, "We consider our work mostly for Hindus and we emphasize this to our students, that each of them is a missionary to witness to his own people."

This theological institution teaches a course entitled "Hinduism and Evangelism" which might help to focus the attention on evangelizing Hindus. However, books on church growth and church planting are not yet studied in this course. And, while all students are given some practical work, not one of them is yet, through the work of the Hindustan Bible Institute, actually planting churches.

Dr. W. D. Coleman, the principal of Andhra Christian Theological College, made the following suggestions under question number eleven:

(a) "There should be a new project to teach evangelism among non-Christians."

(b) "I believe that the Ashram type of appraoch for men and women now being experimented with will bring good results."

(c) "We are planning 'in-service' training for pastors as well as refresher courses with a view to teaching better methods of approach to non-Christians."

For question number eight (see Appendix B), all have said that Hindus are very receptive to the Gospel. For question number ten, the majority of them said that the parish pastor does not have much time for the evangelization of Hindus. They also indicated that he does not have much zeal for such work.

For the last ten years, living in Luthergiri, Rajahmundry, where three theological institutions are situated, I observed the programme of the theological colleges. I also successfully completed the Bachelor of Divinity course in Serampore University. I am sure that the present theological education does not train candidates to disciple Hindus. Moreover, the aim of the programme is to train pastors for the existing churches in Andhra. Very little emphasis, indeed, is laid on communicating the Gospel to those who have yet to believe.

Bishop Lesslie Newbigin helps us see theological education in the larger setting. In an address in South Africa he says:

> For a thousand years, when Christendom was sealed off by Islam from effective contact with the rest of the world, and was contracting, not expanding, it lived in an almost total isolation from non-Christian cultures.
>
> In this situation, the illusion that the age of missions is over became almost an integral part of Christianity. The perpetuation of that illusion is revealed in our normal church life, in the forms of our congregations and parishes, in our conception of the ministry, and in the ordinary consciousness of churchmen.
>
> Our theological curicula bear eloquent testimony

> to this illusion. Our church history is normally taught not as the story of the triumphs of the gospel but as the story of the internal quarrels of the church: our systems of dogmatics are not directed toward the non-Christian faith. The training of the ministry is not for a mission to the world but almost exclusively for the pastoral care of established Christian congregations. (1960:7)

In Andhra, we have three Bible schools for women: Mangalmandiram in Guntur, Charlotte Swenson Memorial Bible Training School at Rajahmundry, and the Canadian Baptist Bible School near Kakinada. These institutions are serving to train Bible women and voluntary workers. As we have seen in chapter three, Bible women have played a very important part in communicating the Gospel to the Hindus.

If women can be trained to communicate Christ to the receptive middle castes of Andhra province, men can be trained too. The total programme of theological education in Andhra needs to be changed to make it indigenous and relevant to the present amazing receptivity among the caste Hindus. This question needs immediate action. The responsible church bodies should institute this change immediately.

I am much impressed with the process of leadership development in New Guinea where Missouri Synod Lutherans are engaged in a tremendous church multiplying programme. I collected this information from reading about this work and especially from interviews with the Rev. Erwin L. Spruth on January 15, 1970 and February 19, 1970. (pastor Spruth served as an evangelistic missionary in New Guinea from 1953 to 1963 at which time he was assigned as Counsellor for Evangelism and Stewardship of the Wabag Lutheran Church. During 1969-70, he was on leave in the United States of America attending the School of World Mission and Institute of Church Growth at Fuller Theological Seminary, working towards a Master's Degree in Missions). On many occasions, he explained how the Gospel is being transmitted by the new members. A few factors involved in his system for developing leaders are: The Missouri Synod of the Lutheran Church in America began work among the Enga people of the Western Highlands of the Territory of New

Guinea in August, 1948. They established Wabag Lutheran Church which by 1970 had a total membership of 38,000 baptized people.

The Catechumenate

> Systematic instruction of properly enrolled classes of catechumens commenced at Yaramanda in 1949, at Irelya in 1951, at Yaibos in 1953, at Sirunki in 1954, and at Papayuk in 1955. Classes of catechumens have also been organized at a number of outstations by the New Guinean missionaries. Instruction is in Bible History and Christian Doctrine, with strong emphasis both on the personal application of what is heard to the faith and life of the catchumens, and on retelling it to others. The catechumens are, according to their abilities, drawn in at an early stage into the witnessing programme, and given continual opportunities, both on the main stations and in many outlying communities, to tell and apply the Bible stories they learn. Thus the concept of Christianity as a thing not only to be held but to be shared becomes firmly established from the very beginning. (Willard Burce, 1955:6)

Catechumens, especially those who have leadership abilities, go to Engas in other areas and communicate the Gospel. The Engas to whom they go, will provide them with their food. After catechumens are baptized, they continue going to these other Enga groups and witnessing to the Lord. They become leaders and start churches wherever they go among various sub-sections of their caste or tribe.

The key principle is that elders out of each ethnic unit becoming Christian are elected and entrusted with a number of responsibilities.

> Almost from the very beginning, at least in some congregations, the Engas have elected elders to whom is entrusted, among other things, the administration of the sacraments. In some congregations, the elders have only been appointed to assist the missionary. This means that they help with the distribution of the Lord's Supper, take care of emergency baptism, and

> perform the baptism* of infant children of Christians. Sometimes the elders applying the water repeats the formula and at other times this is pronounced by the missionary. Sometimes the elder so delegated also gives Communion to the missionary. (Spruth 1960:6)

Our fellow Lutherans in New Guinea are certainly practising "the priesthood of all believers," and as a result are finding natural and efficient leaders. In an interview Pastor Spruth says,

> It is a Church which has grown because the people themselves have been interested in telling others about their Lord Jesus. Together with the Lutheran Mission, the Church is engaged in programmes of education, medical aid, and economic development.

The Development of a New Leadership Programme

I would like to propose a leadership programme which I feel could be developed at once at Luthergiri, Rajahmundry. In the year 1971, Andhra Christian Theological College is moving from Luthergiri, Rajahmundry to Secunderabad. This will leave in Luthergiri a forty-five acre campus with many facilities; a perfect place to develop a programme intended to train multi-level leadership for hundreds of emerging churches in the middle castes. While Andhra Christian Theological College and Gurukal Theological College train pastors on the Licentiate of Theology and Bachelor of Divinity levels, pastors and lay leaders of new Sudhra parishes can be trained on other levels at Luthergiri.

Pastors. To start congregations in the caste sections of our Lutheran Church area, we want to train many pastors. We need to develop new congregations and new pastors simultaneously. The natural leaders should be invited to volunteer for this task. As converts become available, they should be

*This actually is a right of every Christian and does not have to be delegated to anyone special. Cf. Synodical Catechism, page 172 and page 247. Also see F. Peiper, Christian Dogmatics, Vol. III (Concordia Publishing House, St. Louis, 1953), page 279.

selected for this ministry. Christians with zeal in evangelizing non-Christians must be called for this special ministry.

The syllabus of study should include much "church growth" material adapted to modern India. During the training period, the candidates are to be given practical experience in church planting. They would be placed in charge of several house churches. It will be good to follow the Nevius method at least in the beginning. That means these pastors will be paid and will, depending on their ability, supervise maybe ten to forty congregations or house churches, each led by an unpaid local man or women. The size of the house churches and the distance between them will help determine how many a given pastor can supervise.

The pastor is like a spiritual father, but the actual running of the congregation will be entrusted to unpaid leaders. From the very beginning even when they are catechumens, every member not only learns but shares with others what he or she learns. We practise this method in my Ashram. Thus the whole house church is involved in witnessing and worshipping. While doing so, specially gifted people will rise to the leadership. This is the way that works among Hindus. As a group participates in religious activities, some individuals show marked talents. The others naturally accept them as their leaders. Since they have willingly accepted them, they follow them with great respect. Some among these leaders rise to the status of guru and are accepted as spiritual guides. We will do well to follow the same indigenous pattern as we develop Christian leaders.

The Tent-Makers

Along with the full-time pastors, we need to train great numbers of part-time ministers. The concept is relatively new in India but the pattern is firmly rooted in the New Testament and derives its name from Paul who himself was a maker of tents, earning his own living as he preached the Gospel. Dr. Douglas Webster made a survey of the part-time ministry in four different countries and noted a number of benefits this ministry has in his book "Patterns of Part-Time Ministry in Some Churches in South America."

This system should work well with middle class Indians. Most of them have lands to cultivate for their maintenance, some of them would be glad to work as Christian gurus instead of Hindu gurus. Many of them are getting jobs in education or government.

Unpaid Lay Ministry

Arrangements should be made at Luthergiri to train lay men and women especially for voluntary service. The Christian Church started its course through the witness and activity of ordinary people. Most of the companions of St. Paul were dedicated lay people (Acts 18:26, 21:9; Romans 16). The word laity is derived from the Greek word "laos" which means "the people of God." To make the church self-supporting, and self-propagating, large numbers of this kind of church leaders who will arise from the middle castes, are essential.

Theological Education by Extension

Theological training by extension, instead of bringing a few highly educated youth to a seminary, is capable of taking quality training to the deacons, and elders, and tent-making ministers, village pastors, and unpaid local leaders of the Church. It creates courses both to fit the generally lower education of most such leaders as well as courses to fit highly trained lawyers, doctors, and government servants who are found in a few favoured churches. It aims to give education enough so that unpaid lay leaders who are earnest Christians in, say, five or ten years, can meet the requirements for ordination if this seems desirable. It organizes existing pastors and teachers out across the Church to train local leaders. The basic difference between this and residential training is that extension takes theological education into the life schedule of the real leaders of the congregations rather than requiring them to conform to the institutional schedule of a residential school.

This kind of leadership training has worked successfully in Latin America. Mr. Peter Wagner, professor at George

Allan Theological Seminary, Bolivia, explained with great enthusiasm how well their seminary is carrying on this programme with 145 students on four different academic levels (interview on February 5, 1970). He said that the extension movement on the part of all denominations in Latin America now reaches 2,500 ministerial candidates who have registered for courses in 1970.

The Guatemala Plan

This new programme began in 1962 with a Presbyterian seminary in Guatemala, and now includes over 60 other schools in Latin America. In Brazil an association of schools promoting the extension training of ministers began in 1967 with thirty eight schools as charter members.

In Guatemala this movement began in 1962 with 7 candidates and an enrollment in 1968 was 220. The successful functioning of the Guatemala plan depended on three important features of the student-professor-textbook relationship.

The seminary was decentralized into twelve regional centres throughout the territory served by the Presbyterian Church in Guatemala. In each centre, ministerial candidates from nearby congregations met weekly for three hours with one or more itinerant professors from the seminary. Each extension centre had a minimal reference library, a blackboard, maps, and other teaching or learning aids. All the students from the twelve extension centres met once a month for a weekend together at the main campus of the seminary. At these retreats, they had time for interaction with each other, general inspiration, council with their professors, lectures of special interest, and opportunity for study in a well-equipped research library.

Dr. Ralph Winter, one of the developers of this new decentralized approach, enumerates twelve discoveries that arose out of this programme. I would mention seven of them.

> 1. Students and even faculty whose existence we had never noticed before now seemingly appeared out of nowhere. Our full-time faculty of five now had the part-time help of twelve others who could serve in

weekly and monthly meetings.

2. The extension centres allowed us to reach up to higher as well as down to lower academic levels than we had operated before.

3. We found we could train men right where they were without pulling them out of their own local environment, and that we could thus reach at least five different subcultures with the same institution.

4. We found that studying by extension was a good deal tougher, and that we had unintentionally designed a vast screening programme gathering men who not only had talent but also personal discipline.

5. Some criticism arose that we were closing the door to the ministry to younger men. A check showed we had more younger men than ever despite an average age in the thirties.

6. We maintained precisely the same curriculum as we had used through the years, but we found our new breed of students doing better work than ever—partly due to the new kind of books, mainly due to their greater maturity. Furthermore, a man who is successful in extension studies builds personal study habits that will serve him the rest of his life.

7. The programme cost far less per student. At one point, when we still had both residential and extension students, we found we were spending roughly 70 per cent of our budget for five students living in and 30 per cent for 65 in extension studies. Same for teacher energies. (1969:308,309)

Dr. F. Ross Kinsler of the seminary gives some practical insights into the success of the new programme with a penetrating analysis of its ten 1967 graduates. Their average age was 37.6. They all had a number of years in secular employment (average 14.2 years), averages 8.2 years of secular education, and they had had abundant "practical work" in the church, averaging 8.3 years as follows:

By the time they finished their studies three of the ten were already ordained pastors, three paid church "workers," three ruling elders, and one a Bible Institute teacher. Only one expects to serve the church outside the ordained ministry. (Kinsler 1967)

James E. Hill (1969:221) points out four salient features in this new theological programme.

> (1) It was a bold attempt to bring theological education closer to the New Testament ideal of the ministry. (2) It was a radical departure from the traditional resident seminary programme. (3) It demonstrated daring confidence in the ability of dedicated, mature men to discipline themselves to a rigorous self-study programme. (4) It reflected an unusual display of missionary courage and hardwork in the production of programmed texts and the setting up of an entirely new seminary structure that continues to function successfully, at this point with only one missionary on the central faculty.

The Pentecostal Ministry in Chile

The case of the growth of an indigenous ministry in the Pentecostal churches of Chile is another remarkable example of the development of proficiency outside traditional structure of theological education. This programme has been documented by the World Council of Churches observer, Christian La Live D'Epinay. He describes their system in the following manner:

> The Pentecostalist system has two essential characteristics; every convert is an evangelist;...and every convert can, if he shows that he has the gift... one day be entrusted with pastoral responsibilities. But this takes a long time and the neophyte has to climb the rungs if the hierarchical ladder one by one. Soon after his conversion he starts as a preacher in the street, where he proves the depth of his convictions and quality of his witness. He will then be given responsibility for a Sunday school class and will accede to the status of preacher; he will then have the right to lead worship. (D'Epinay 1967:Vol.56,188)

The general feeling about Pentecostalism in the past was that the movement was greatly lacking in theological education. But D'Epinay draws our attention to the fact that the

Pentecostal system is strong where other Protestant churches are typically weak:

> The Pentecostalist system corrects all the defects in the Protestant system in the developing countries. It draws its recruits from the widest possible field; any member of the church can become a pastor, if he is converted at an advanced age. It gives members a collective responsibility, drawing everyone into evangelism . . . finally, it produces pastors who are the genuine expression of the congregation, since they do not differ from them either socially or culturally. We are convinced that this system of pastoral training is an important factor in the success of Pentecostalism . . (D'Epinay 1967:Vol.56,190)

Many of the insights that D'Epinay sighted regarding ministerial training are very helpful in training leaders for the house church that I am proposing for converts.

Long before I came to the School of World Mission, I had done some thinking along the line of extension seminary education. In 1968, I sent out a questionnaire to fifty-nine Lutheran pastors asking them whether they would like to open a centre in their parish to train voluntary Christian workers. Fifty-five said "yes," one said "no," and three did not return the questionnaire. In October, 1968, I submitted the following suggestion to the Long Range Planning Conference: That the three Bible training institutes conduct programmes at different centres to train leaders.

As I do more study on the subject, I am convinced that theological education by extension will solve many problems in getting the proper leadership for evangelizing the large Hindu population of Andhra.

The theological training programme that we start at Luthergiri must definitely include producing these causes according to this new pattern of training leaders. It is not possible for many of the middle class men and women to leave their homes and work and go to some distant centre for long periods of time for training. In their culture and economy, it is neither common or possible for adults to go to school. To become Christians is already a big step. On top of that to ask them to go away for three years or more years of special training is in almost all cases too much. Moreover, they know of men among themselves who educate themselves and develop "naturally" into quite acceptable gurus. It would fit in very well with what they know, if the lay leaders of the congregations in the Hindu sections of the villages were trained by teachers from among themselves working in their midst by extension methods.

7

The New Role of the Missions Today in Andhra

The Need for the Missions

Missions are required in Andhra as long as there are winnable people who need to come to Christ. But all missions should work more in evangelism ahead-of-the church and outside of existing congregations, and less in the existing churches. If we get too tied up with existing churches, we are susceptible to the Church's saying, "We do not need any more missionaries," This may be true for existing Christians but not true for the multitudes who have yet to come to the Lord. Bishop Newbigin makes the following statement which is applicable to all the denominations and Churches of Andhra.

> The conclusion would then seem to be that in a few years' time we could withdraw all missionaries from India. The logic is impeccable. What is wrong is the starting point. While 97 per cent of India remains non-Christian, and probably 80 per cent out of touch with the Gospel, what missionary logic can permit us to say "the task is done and missionaries can be withdrawn."
>
> It is the Indian Church itself which is challenging this way of thinking. More and more Indian Christian leaders are saying: The thing the missionary should bring us is not primarily his technical expertness, it

> is his missionary passion. We want missionaries above all to help us to go outside ourselves and bring Christ to our people. This then is the missionary's task today. (Newbigin 1960:23)

The present churches in Andhra will not be able to evangelize the enormous numbers of Hindus. As we know, Christians form only a small percentage of the total population. Most of them have been "receiving" churches for too long a period. We cannot expect them to become missionary-minded overnight. First of all, they do not quite realize the need for the outreach. The churches for the most part, have become introverted—concerned with their own needs only. they do not hear their Lord's call to disciple the hundreds of non-Christian ethne. On the other hand, Christians want the missions still to support what they call "church work" with all its internal administration and institutions. In some cases, Christians might even object to the missions having special evangelization programmes for non-Christians.

Gilbert Olson's fine study of church growth in Sierra Leone, the oldest Protestant mission field in Africa, has the following illuminating passage.

> Bishop Stephen Neill asks a penetrating question which every mission board—and emerging national leadership—ought to ask when devolution is being considered, or after it already has taken place: But what is to happen, if a younger Church fails to rise to the heights of its responsibilities, and to take the initiative in setting evangelistic work in motion. Bishop Neill recognizes the problems involved but does not hesitate to speak clearly what he believes to be the mind of God:
>
> "... younger Church leaders sometimes give the impression that they would rather their fellow-countrymen die as heathens than that they should be brought to the knowledge of Christ by Christians from the West. If such a situation is reached, then there is nothing for it but the older Churches to rebel. A dictatorship of the younger Churches is no better than a dictatorship of the missionary societies. Partnership is not a human alliance for mutual convenience, it is partnership

> in obedience to the command of Christ to preach the Gospel to every creature. If this obedience is lacking on one side or the other, the partnership would seem to lack a valid foundation. The world situation is changing so rapidly that opportunities are being lost every day. If an older Church seems to hear the clear call to evangelize, it may be necessary that it should go forward, leaving the younger Church to follow when it is sufficiently awake itself to hear the call (1957)." (1969:109)

The goal of the missions is not to serve the existing churches only. Doing that runs the risk of becoming an end in itself and cripples the effectiveness of the missions. The goal is to disciple every person who is waiting to hear the Good News. To start new churches among Hindus is the primary task of all the missions in Andhra. No slavery to "indigenous principles" should come in the way of carrying on the great Commission of the Lord.

> In Cameroon, the missionaries were so devoted to "indigenous" principles that they refused to evangelize a new and receptive tribe on the ground that the nationals should do it. When indigenous principles interfere with completing the Great Commission, or prevent the salvation of some, they should be scrapped. (Wagner :unpublished material)

Dr. McGavran, while discussing indigenous church principles, draws our attention to the important task of foreign missions.

> Henry Venn of the English Church Missionary Society and Rufus Anderson of the American Board of Commissioners for Foreign Missions both advocated what would today be called indigenous church principles. Anderson wrote, "The grand object of foreign missions is to plant and multiply churches, composed of native converts, each church complete in itself, with presbyters of the same race, left to determine their ecclesiastical relations for themselves, with the aid of judicious advice from their missionary fathers." (McGavran 1970:337)

What Catholics are thinking about the missionary activity

is well worth considering. Pius XII says:

> The primary object of missionary activity, as every one knows, is to bring the shining light of Christian truth to new peoples and to form new Christians. To attain, however, this object, the ultimate one, missionaries must unremittingly endeavour to establish the Church firmly among other peoples and to endow them with their own native hierarchy (Evangelii Praecones:32) (Luzbetak 1970:105)

Evangelism is no doubt the function of the Church, but it is even more fundamentally the function of the missionary, the mission, and the division of the world mission. There is danger that evangelism becomes the activity of nationals only. A significant proportion of missionary staff and budget should be assigned to evangelism.

> The primary aim of the mission was always to be widespread evangelism. The shepherding of Churches and education could be undertaken, but not to such an extent as to hide or hinder the one central and commanding purpose. (Neill (1964) 1966:334)

The Duties of the Missions in Pioneer Church Planting

This is the heart of the matter. Should missions in Andhra in all of their programmes work only through existing churches? Or can they on occasion act independently, especially when doing pioneer work such as evangelizing caste Hindus? For many solid reasons, right from the beginning, all missions should plant indigenous churches among the Hindus so that they might take care of themselves in a short period of time and also help to plant churches in as yet unevangelized portions of their community.

For the last hundred years and more, missions have greatly assisted young churches rising out of the Harijan communities. For this we can thank God. More than anything else, this work of missions has benefitted India and helped to remove the stain of "untouchability." All this is good.

But it is now time for the missions to make available to middle castes and other Hindus some of the same inestim-

able benefit of knowing Jesus Christ and forming living churches.

Up to this point, I have been speaking about missions in general. Now let me turn specifically to our own church situation.

Specific Opportunity for the Board of World Missions of the Lutheran Church in America

Fortunately, the Board of World Missions through its executive, Dr. J. F. Neudoerffer, has formulated a comprehensive statement of the situation.

> There are three possible alignments of responsibility of three categories into which . . . programmes may fall. The first is that of AEL Church responsibility alone. Herein would be included those programmes which the AEL Church feels compelled to carry on without any involvement at all from the Home Board. Such programmes are initiated, financed, and carried through by the AELC itself.
>
> The second is that of AELC-BWM joint responsibility. Such a programme, conceived by either of agencies would involve both AELC and BWM in the planning, financing, staffing and carrying out the programme with a prior agreement that the BWM will phase out after a stipulated time after which the programme shall be the full responsibility of the AEL Church or to be renegotiated for a further period of time.
>
> The third is that of the BWM responsibility. Such a programme, conceived by either the BWM or AELC, upon prior agreement, would be operated by the BWM within the boundaries of or contiguous to the boundaries of the AELC. In such a programme, the AELC could choose whether it wanted to join with the BWM or not but in any case the BWM would operate the programme on a short term basis after which the programme would either be turned over to the AELC or would be left to become self-supporting or even possibly be abandoned. (Neudoerffer 1968:6)

Dr. Neudoerffer's third alignment is precisely what I have had in mind for many years. Let the Andhra Evangelical Lutheran Church turn this matter of pioneer mission to the Hindus over to the Board of World Missions. In some places, the Andhra Evangelical Lutheran Church might wish to join forces with this pioneer mission effort. And if it does so, it will be most welcome. But the burden, the annual cost, the travailling with new Christians and new churches "till Christ be formed in them" will be the primary responsibility of the Board of World Missions.

The Board of World Missions, as its part, should plan to rear self-supporting churches. The burden of the new congregations should be temporary. As early as possible the new churches should go forward under their own leaders—chiefly lay, but also clerical—paying all their own expenses.

Furthermore, all the new insights as to church growth in homogeneous units should be utilized in this new pioneer evangelism. New churches should be encouraged to be church planters.

The Continuing Responsibility of the Existing Church

The Existing Church has a glowing opportunity and primary responsibility to disciple the non-Christians in its own cultural and ethnic community, namely Harijans. It is tragic but alas it is true that most Christians are not as concerned about the salvation of their own kith and kin as one might wish. There are large numbers of Harijans who live next door to the Christians and who are their own relatives and friends.

For existing Christians to reach the caste areas is difficult, but they should certainly be able to evangelize their own people. We should not say that the remainder of the Harijans are a resistant population and forget about them. God is interested in saving them. All efforts should be expended to investigate the reasons for their indifference to Christianity and ways found to open the door of eternal life to them.

In recent years, the Rev. P. Y. Luke and John B. Carman made a survey of some Christian congregations in Medak Diocese, Andhra. They found out that many Harijans are not becoming Christians for the following reasons.

> ....three of the five congregations especially studied were largely of entirely Madiga in background, and (that) the Malas in these villages have been unwilling to accept Christianity because they feared they would then have to live in the congregation with Madigas, accepting them as equals. The Malas in their villages claim to be unable to notice any difference in the conduct of the Madigas since they became Christian. Moreover, at the present time they fear that to become Christians, would mean losing the benefits they have been receiving as Harijans. (1968:147)

It is the responsibility of the Church to go into these and many other problems that the Harijans are facing and help them to become disciples of the Lord.

It may well be that as the Church spreads among the middle castes, the pagan reservoir among the Harijans will become more responsive. Indeed in God's providence, it may be that (to apply Romans 11:25) a temporary "hardening has come upon part of" the Harijans "until the full number of the" cast Hindus "have come in." (Romans 11.25)

Thus, Mission and Church will work together, each at its appointed task, for the glory of God and the expansion of His Kingdom.

8

Recommendations

In this thesis, I have made many practical proposals. Others have been implied. Now I would like to summarize them in the form of seventeen recommendations to the Lutheran Church and Mission.

1. Research Project in Andhra Pradesh:

The different Churches in Andhra are carrying on various programmes of evangelism. It will pay us to survey these. One such survey—of Lutheran evangelism—has already been done in the Lutheran Church by the Rev. S. W. Schmitthenner. If we survey the whole province at least in broad outlines, we shall get a more complete picture of the Christian approach to Hindus in Andhra. I feel the findings of such a research provide us with proper guidelines to proceed with the important task of discipling Hindus. I have drawn a research design (see Appendix D).

I recommend that the Board of World Missions of the Lutheran Church in America sponsor this study.

2. Training Five Kinds of Leaders:

To train five kinds of leaders needed by growing churches is an urgent matter. Let me say a word about each kind.

(a) Unpaid local leaders concerned with the inner life of the congregation. We need a large number of these leaders for the present congregations as well as for the new ones. There are many natural leaders. We do well by training such.

Among Hindus, many keep busy with religious activities on a voluntary basis. All the year round, local leaders celebrate many festivals. Basing on the same pattern, leaders can be developed in the Christian Churches.

(b) Unpaid leaders concerned with the propagation of the Gospel. In India, the social structure is such that people in one village or town have relatives and friends in many other villages and towns. They know how to "gossip the Gospel." Men and women take great pleasure in telling others what they know about and value most. As in Western countries, one does not need to have an appointment or a formal interview to get information, especially from people in rural areas. They make it their business to tell everybody they come in contact with and especially their kith and kin. During our Ashram, some women walked long distances to tell the Good News to their relatives. In many cases, they succeeded in interesting them in the Gospel.

Most of the people whom we can call leaders, do not have much education. They need help to understand the Scriptures. They are anxious to sing, but have little opportunity to learn Christian songs. They need to be taught the fundamentals of the Christian faith.

(c) Paid leaders of village churches, recruited largely from the adult village Christians, i.e., from those becoming Christians.

As the voluntary workers spread the news, there is need for organizing Christians into congregations. For this purpose and also to give the day-to-day spiritual care to the faithful members, some paid ordained and unordained leaders are essential. Adequate training must be given to these candidates.

(d) Paid preachers who serve in large urban congregations or supervise village congregations. The urban situation demands especially qualified ministers. Better educated Christians in the pews need better educated ministers in the

pulpit. More and more people are moving to towns and cities; competent leadership must be developed to meet the need.

(e) Highly educated leaders of marked ability who occupy notable administrative and teaching posts. Every denomination needs a few of these remarkably capable and devoted persons.

We need all the above five classes of leaders in our Church to implement the new programme, I recommend that the first three types of leaders (men and women) be trained in Luthergiri and that the last two can be trained in Andhra Christian Theological College and in Gurukul Research Institute.

3. Church Growth Through Theological Education

The Theological Institutions must graduate candidates who are successful at church planting, In order to achieve this goal, candidates, while they are in training, should be given experience in starting new congregations.

Singapore Bible College has been very successful in leading students to plant churches. The Rev. E. N. Poulson, the dean of Singapore College, says,

> . . . these socially unsettled thousands of people are winnable. . . . Each high rise building has about 1,200 occupants. We believe a church (congregation) can be planted right in the building where people live. More than half a dozen such churches have emerged as a result of intensive door-to-door evangelism within each building. In some instances, services have been held in the flat of the believer. At least three worshipping groups are housed in a ground floor shop. (CGB, January, 1970:45)

Singapore Bible College runs an evening Bible course for all kinds of professional people. In conversation with me, Mr. Poulson said,

> From the very first, the training of full-time students in the Singapore Bible College has been supplemented by an extensive evening school in which enrollment has, at times, reached as high as 200 businessmen and professionals. (Interview on February 8, 1970)

It is encouraging to note that the Singapore Bible College gets most of its financial support from the local people. Mr. Poulson remarked, "We are a spiritual blessing to the people and they support us."

I recommend that our theological institutes train church planters and have close relationship with the community.

4. Theological Education By Extension

We have found out that the American and British structures for ministerial training are not fully adequate for the younger churches.

> The plumb line must be, "Are these graduates adapting themselves to the local people whom they understand and with whom they can work to produce soul-winning churches"? The end result of a (theological) training programme must be the planting and expanding of churches. If the training is producing other than soul-winning, church building graduates, it is missing its mark. (Scanlon 1962:25)

Vernon A. Reimer (quoted by Savage) makes the following valid statement.

> Some students from the rural churches, having received several years of institute training, experience difficulty in adjusting themselves to the humble life of the community to which they minister, feeling that to adapt themselves to the lowly customs of the villagers would be a step down for them. Nor do they fit into the urban church situation. (Savage 1969:67,68)

Instead of the students adjusting to the institution, it is better if the institution can adjust to the students. Theological education by extension is found to be successful wherever it is started.

The George Allan Theological Seminary, Cochabamba, Bolivia, trains four levels of theological students through extension programmes. Missionary John A. Vigus, who has been teaching in their seminary for the last five years, gave a very encouraging report about the progress of the programme (Interview on January 24, 1970).

Missionary Paul Enyart works in Berea Bible Institute,

Chiquimula (Central America) which trains pastoral leadership by extension programmes. He says,

> I feel the extension programme is the wave of the future in theological education, and the future growth of the churches will depend greatly on how flexible their theological programme is in meeting the challenge of preparing local church leadership. (Interview on February 10, 1970)

He gave a number of examples where the graduates, by extension course, are doing better work than those in their residential programme.

In the Indian situation, it is important that we start this programme. Many of the middle class people will not be able to come to the institutions for the training, If we have only the institutional training, we shall lose many efficient leaders. Moreover, extension is the most economic way to train leaders, and thus the earliest to become fully indigenous in control.

My recommendation is that we start multi-level training programmes at Luthergiri and that the same organization take care of the extension programme also.

5. Establishment of the House Churches Among Converts:

At present, in many places we have prayer cells consisting mainly of women, They can be converted into small congregations. The smallness of the house church should not concern us. Let us remember our Lord's words, "Where two or three gathered, there I am.." (Matthew 18:20) These nucleus groups of Christians have a chance of influencing larger groups of non-Christians. Dr. Tippett, in a personal interview, said:

> In Fiji, it is the extended family that influences the lineage, among the Anuaks of Ethiopia the Church grows in an "age grade," in some societies it begins with an occupational class as with the Port Fanti in Gold Coast and in others it may begin with women's groups or maybe men's groups. Thus, the small group is the bridge into the big group. It may be for a time that the Church grows in the small group only. But

> the small group must never lose sight of its responsibility to win the larger group. This is easier for them to do than the foreign missionary. (Interview on February 16, 1970)

No more time should be wasted. We should immediately follow the New Testament pattern of house churches. I strongly recommend that the Board of World Missions take initiative to implement the programme to start house churches among the Hindus.

6. Ordination for Different Levels of Preachers.

The Lutheran doctrine of "the priesthood of all believers" and the Scriptures encourage us to ordain candidates of various levels of theological training. Bishop Azariah set a very good example by ordaining village workers.

> When Vedanayakam Samuel Azariah was consecrated in 1912 as the first Indian bishop of the Anglican Church in India, he found himself in charge of a large area in which a mass movement was in progress. This he guided with consummate skill through thirty years, helped by the support of a number of exceptionally able and self-effacing European missionaries. Throughout the whole period the number of baptisms averaged 3,000 a year. Azariah followed the practice that had been familiar to him in his own boyhood days in Tinnevelly; as soon as possible, village workers who had approved themselves as catechists were brought forward, and, in spite of defective general and theological education, were ordained to the priesthood of the Church. Educational standards were steadily raised, and by the end of his time Azariah was ordaining men who were graduates both in arts and in theology.
>
> The policy of the Methodists in the adjoining area of Medak, where their great pioneer was the Reverend Charles Posnett, was rather different. Holding that there should be as little disparity as possible between the European and the Indian minister, they admitted to ordination only those who had received full theo-

logical training, As a result, fifty years after the beginning of the movement their missionaries still outnumbered their Indian ministers. (Neill 1966:479, 480)

In the light of the experience of these two Churches, we can see our way clearly. I recommend that we ordain different levels of preachers for multiplying congregations among Hindus.

7. Ordination for Women

In Hindu culture, it is difficult for men to evangelize women. Until now, most of the evangelism among Hindu women has been done by women. When we think of establishing churches, it helps a great deal to have some ordained women for this special ministry.

As we know, Lutheran Churches in some countries ordain women. I quote the opinions of some Lutheran leaders.

Bishop W. Westergaard Madsen of Denmark said (Letter February 23, 1970):

> About ordination of women:
> 1) Law of June 4, 1947 gives women access to be ordained, and the first ordination of a woman took place in that year.
> 2) About 30
> 3) Normal pastoral work.
> 4) There are in the Lutheran Church different opinions about the ordination of women. The bishops as a whole are willing to ordain women, which means that they think that in this matter of order, the Church has its freedom to organize as the situation demands, but there is in our Church a group of pastors who do think that the Church ought not to ordain women.

In August, 1969, I met a lady pastor, the Rev. Eva Maria Siebert, in Darmstadt, West Germany. She is a very interesting person. She had made complete plans to come to work in the Tamil Lutheran Church in India, but could not get a visa. At present she is in charge of a congreagtion in Darmstadt. She says (Letter of January 6, 1970):

> I like my profession very much. I have no special

> problems because I am a lady-pastor. I am fully accepted by my congregation members in every kind of work—such as conducting services, to give Holy Communion and baptism, to conduct funeral services and matrimonial services.

The Rev. Theo Aschoff, a Lutheran pastor in West Germany wrote (Letter of January 14, 1970): "We have started ordaining women in 1966, the ordained women do various kinds of work."

Some might wonder whether Indian women can be ministers. When an Indian woman is accepted as a Prime Minister of the country, I do not see how anyone can object to an Indian woman becoming a pastor!

My recommendation, therefore, is that at least a few women be ordained for special ministry among the Hindus.

8. An Order for Women:

In the Lutheran Church, for the outreach of the Gospel, the ministry of women is important. If women evangelists and other women were to belong to an organization, it would give them a status in Church and society. Moreover, in India where community life is predominant, every individual is expected to belong to a group.

There are deaconess orders in many countries. Both the Church of South India and the Tamil Evangelical Lutheran Church have an "order of women." By establishing an order, we do not encourage people to stay single, but do recognize the spiritual gift of persons who serve the Lord in that state.

Let us consider the possibilities for understanding singleness as a genuine possibility in Christian vocation, to which God calls people.

Anglican V. A. Demont offers one response:

> The idea of holy virginity is indispensable to the idea of holy matrimony....Marriage can be accepted and embraced as a high vocation only in a world in which there exists some feasible and proper alternative. Without a place for vocational virginity, sexuality and marriage become necessary and cease to be vocational.

Reformed Church theologian Karl Barth points out that marriage in the New Testament "is no longer an absolute, but relative necessity.... Singleness becomes a possibility, a way, a matter of special gift and vocation." Barth points out that Christ was fully man without marriage. He spoke of his brethren, his family, as those who did the will of the Father, and of the kingdom in which there is "neither marriage nor giving in marriage." He also spoke of those who metaphorically made themselves eunuchs for the sake of the kingdom. Barth concluded: "Marriage in the New Testament is obviously relativized; it is neither a high way nor a better possibility for the Christian." The Christian enters marriage on the basis

> ... of a special spiritual gift and vocation within his life history and the history of salvation in the freedom of the Spirit.... The same freedom opens up the possibility of not marrying. Strangely enough, for the married and the unmarried to deny this other possibility and make marriage a universal obligation deprives it of its only meaning for the Christian. There is a genuine Christian obedience which does not lead a person into marriage, but past it. It is the magna carta of all who are unmarried---as long as they understand and exercise their voluntary or involuntary celibacy as a matter of Christian obedience.
> (Subamma 1968:42;43)

Paul spoke of freedom from marital cares and distractions as enabling the single to devote themselves to God's service. Basing on the Scriptures as well as the experience of the Christian Church, to establish "an order for women" in the Churches wherever possible is quite fitting. In a big Church like the Andhra Evangelical Lutheran where a good number of single women are doing service in different capacities, to start some kind of suitable "order for women" as in the Church of South India is essential.

9. New Methods of Evangelism

Evangelism intends to persuade men to become disciples of Christ. Many factors convince us that the non-Christians are more responsive to the Gospel than ever before. But we need a new approach.

Previously we were satisfied mostly with the proclamation of the Gospel. Now we are also interested in planting churches. So I recommend that we adopt new methods in evangelizing Hindus.

10. Ashram Programmes:

Ashram is an indigenous term. It appeals to the Indian mind. During the Ashram programme at Luthergiri, many Hindus and converts voiced their strong opinions that this one should continue and others should be started.

In whatever form, the church can only be a place of worship, it cannot take the place of an ashram. Dr. Winter makes a distinction between these two types of structures.

> ... our modern American parish type of community, which offers a kind of out-patient treatment to the members---once or twice or three times a week. The monastery by comparison is a twenty-four hour military-type settlement where a person---like in residence school---experience a total involvement in life, the kind of movement where you don't win people to Christ, but you invite them in! In many specific situations in mission fields today there are circumstances where we may have to think in terms of a more comprehensive community to which we invite people, lock stock and barrel. Not just temporarily, not just to sweep the corridors and be hangers-on, but invite them into a corporate on-going community that supports itself and moves forward as an independent, permanent structure. (Winter 1969:300. 301)

Ashrams will be effective channels of communicating the Gospel in a natural and effective way. I propose that the Christian Ashram at Luthergiri and the Lydia Ashram at Vadali be continued and ashrams be started in other synods also; and that available mission buildings be used for this purpose.

It is interesting to note that Dr. E. Stanley Jones started the first ashram in America in 1940 and since then, it has multiplied enormously under his leadership.

11. Scripture Distribution:

The number of people who can read has increased enormously in Andhra. In 1951 13.1 per cent could read and in 1961 21.2 per cent were able to read. If we can place a Gospel in the hands of every man and woman who can read, we shall have made it possible for multitudes to begin their inquiry into the Gospel. Narayan Vamana Tilak, Sadu Sunder Singh and many others were convicted through the Living Word of God. People ask me who converted me and I have no better answer than to say "the Word of God."

In many places in Andhra as well as in India, the Bible is accepted better than the preacher. When men and women get interested in "the Book," Christians have more chance of leading them to know the Saviour.

Bible distribution has much to do with the amazing church growth in Brazil. I had an interesting interview with the Rev. Robert A. Orr, missionary to Brazil (Interview, February 26, 1970). He says, "The Bible in the hands of an unbeliever often results in his conversion and this convert is often influential in starting a church. This has taken place over and over again in the past and is still taking place today." He told me how he organizes his programme to reach the people with the Bible and then do so much follow up work,

> Bible circulation before 1914 led the way for today's exciting church growth in Brazil! The American and British Societies began to smuggle Bibles to Brazilian merchants via sailors who were the go-betweens.
>
> The records show that between the two societies 2,900,000 Bibles had been put into circulation in Brazil by 1900. At that time, the population of Brazil was seventeen million. This means that there was a Bible for every six persons or one could say, a Bible for every family on the average. (Orr: unpublished material)

The Bible should always be the basic tool for evangelism and church planting. It will bring lasting results and continued spiritual growth. The Word of God can break down unresponsiveness in many populations and open many doors to the church planter. But we must not stop with Bible distribution: we must go on multiplying congregations among the responsive Kapus, Reddys, Kammas and others.

I recommend that all efforts be made to reach millions of non-Christians with the Scriptures.

12. Outreach Through the Institutions

Ways and means can be investigated to reach non-Christians through the hospitals and schools. Many times first contacts have been made in the hospitals and follow up work should be done in the villages and towns of the grateful patients, There should, of course, be good coordination between the two.

I recommend that an evaluation of the evangelistic outreach through the institutions be done and new methods be instituted for the more effective church planting among Kamma, Reddy, Kapu, and other patients.

13. Indigenous Worship

Indigenous worship using Indian music and native musical instruments must be introduced in the church service. Where ever necessary, changes should be made to suit the standard of the worshippers. The form of worship services can be flexible. The active participation of the members is desirable. A period of silence is also to the taste of Indians. Intelligible terms might be introduced to the benefit of the new Christians.

I recommend that in every way possible, worship must be in Indian patterns. The Hindu must feel at home in the prayer life of the hundreds of home churches which will be begun.

14. Indigenous Literature

The new approach certainly needs many types of literature. New books have to be written for the programme at Luthergiri. There should not be any trouble finding talented people to write. But they must be trained especially in the new methods of approach in the leadership programme and in evangelization.

I recommend that a workshop be convened to train writers.

15. Cultural Heritage

Anthropology is teaching us that it is desirable for each people to keep its own cultural heritage.

There are certain practices in Christian Churches which are not necessary on the basis of Scripture. Moreover, they are great obstacles for Hindus to become Christians. I would like to mention two such.

For no valid reason, the bottu (beauty mark) is prohibited for Christian women in Andhra. I consulted some Hindu pandits and they all said that bottu does not have any religious significance for women. Dr. E. Sambayya, a convert from the highest caste in India (Brahmin) who was principal of Bishop's College and who acted as the president of Serampore College Council for some years, wrote the following statement regarding bottu (letter, Bangalore, dated December 30, 1969).

> In the classical religious tradition of Hinduism, the bottu denoted a woman's married state, and it was discarded when she became a widow.
>
> In the nineteenth century when converts had to leave their house and had to be segregated, they were made to be and to look as different as possible from this previous state. Discarding of bottu was intended to highlight this clean break with the past; and there was some justification for it under those circumstances.
>
> But in context of the ongoing Hindu culture which is rapidly evolving, bottu has acquired a non-religious significance as a part of the woman's facial makeup. It became a beauty mark, and an element in the facial decoration. Thus, some of the fashionable Muslim women also wore it occasionally for parties.
>
> In North India, young Christian women usually wore bottu as a part of their "getting dressed" for the day. South India is more conservative. But the practice

> is widespread now all over India. My daughter always wore it. Usha was married with it. So was Meera. There is no Scriptural basis either for wearing it or for discarding it. What matters in the Bible is the love for God and our concern for man.

Since Dr. Sambayya was an orthodox Hindu and theologian, his word must be respected.

Another disturbing Christian tradition is burying the dead. Among most Hindus, cremation is accepted as the symbol of status. Among Hindus only certain castes---and these usually are the poorest---prefer burial. Some families object to becoming Christian because of the "Christian" custom of burying the dead.

Many other changes in Christian customs to make them fit the culture of the middle castes might be mentioned, but space will not permit. In my questionnaire is this question (See Appendix C, Numer 3), "Should we make cultural changes even if these seem strange and, at first glance, undesirable to older Christians"? I distributed this to thirty-five missionaries from twenty-six countries representing eleven denominations who were studying at the School of World Mission and Institute of Church Growth. They answered the following ways. Twenty-eight said "definitely yes." Four did not answer. Three gave indefinite answers. This indicates that an overwhelming majority of missionaries from many countries and many different backgrounds see the need for change. They agree that if the Church and her leaders do not make these changes, the spread of the Gospel will be greatly hindered.

I recommend that these and other traditions which do not have any biblical basis should not be made compulsory for the converts to observe. The Gospel should be able to be accepted without needless, unnecessary culture change.

16. The Church's Responsibility to Evangelize Harijans and Other Hindus

The Andhra Evangelical Lutheran Church has received much blessing for over a century and a quarter. It is her turn now to share her blessings. Our Church must feel the

responsibility not merely to urge the Board to undertake the pioneer work I have described, but herself to disciple Harijans who are her next door neighbours. She also must cooperate to evangelize caste people as much as she can.

My recommendation is that the Church find new ways of discipling Harijans.

17. Board of World Missions Implementation of the New Approach to Hindus

As we have already seen, the existing Andhra Evangelical Lutheran Church, for many reasons, cannot effectively carry on the widespread discipling of the Sudhras which is now possible. The Board of World Missions as a World Church can pioneer this difficult task in which so many new steps need to be taken. For a short time, personnel and finance should be provided by the Board. A significant proportion of missionary staff and budget should be assigned to disciple the non-Christians.

We may not find all the needed personnel in the Lutheran Church. Trained leaders can be borrowed from other Churches in Andhra or from the member churches of the Federation of Lutheran Churches in India. In these days when it is becoming difficult to secure visas for missionaries, we do well by exchanging personnel with India.

Even more important than new missionaries and workers, are the new ways of evangelizing and forming churches. Permission should be given to try out many new policies, new departures, and new methods. The exciting and dangerous new ways of spreading the Gospel to the receptive portions of the ethnic units in modern India should not be confined by rules and regulations laid down in the nineteenth century.

I recommend that the Board of World Missions courageously take the opportunity to disciple Hindus in Andhra Pradesh. I am sure that the Andhra Evangelical Lutheran Church will rejoice in this aid and welcome these new resources.

CONCLUSION

I would like to conclude my thesis with the Great Commission of our Lord (Matthew 28:19-20, Phillips edition).

> All power in Heaven and on earth has been given to me. You, then, are to go and make disciples of all the nations and baptize them in the name of the Father and of the Son and of the Holy Spirit. Teach them to observe all that I have commanded you and, remember, I am with you always, even to the end of the world.

APPENDICES

Appendix A

Dear Friends:

I am studying in Fuller Theological Seminary and my research is entitled, "A Christian Approach to Hindus." I shall be most grateful if you will give me the following information required for my thesis:

QUESTIONNAIRE (denomination, not Church)

1. What is the baptized membership of your church?........
2. How many caste converts are now in your church?.......
3. How many from tribal background (like Koya, Lambadi, etc.) are members?..........................
4. Do you have special workers like Bible women and Evangelists to evangelize Hindus?............
5. Do all converts attend church or Sunday worship?.....

   or

   Do they often meet separately for prayers on Sunday?....
6. Should converts always attend the church which is in the Christian locality?.................

   Or, do you know of circumstances in which separate services would be desirable?................
7. From among the converts, are there any trained pastors and evangelists?....................

   How many?....................................
8. Do such persons preach the Gospel to Hindus?..........
9. Do you see any advantage of training and using such personnel..........................
10. Are Hindus these days responsive to the Gospel?.......
11. Any further information concerning work among Hindus?..................................

....

Signature:..................Designation..................Denomination

May I request you kindly to reply on this sheet and send to Miss Solomon at the address below, and she will mail it to me.

Miss L. A. Solomon, Headmistress & Correspondent, Shade School, Rajahmundry-3, Andhra Pradesh.

Thank you.

Yours sincerely,
B. V. Subbamma

BVS:fj

(Miss) B. V. Subbamma

P.S. Even if you do not have all the information, please send what is available, as early as possible . . . . since I need it soon.

Appendix B

B. V. Subbamma
(Principal, Bible Training School, Rajahmundry)
135 North Oakland Avenue
Pasadena, California 91101, U. S. A.

Questionnaire to Theological Seminaries & Bible Training Institutes:

1. Name of the Institution
2. Number of staff Students Duration
3. What workers do you train?
4. What subjects in your curriculum focus the attention on evangelizing Hindus?
5. What kind of practical Evangelistic work do you do among Hindus?
6. What are the methods used?
7. How is the follow-up work taken care of?
8. Do you think that Hindus are responsive to the Gospel?
9. Do you see any new possibilities of carrying on Evangelism among Hindus through your institution?
10. Do you feel that the parish pastor has the urge to do Evangelistic work among Hindus?
    Does he have time to do this ministry?
11. Please make your suggestions on the following items:
    (a) Introducing subjects in your curriculum to encourage your students to evangelize:

(b) Give cases of practical work which really brings results:

(c) Can your institution arrange seminars for Pastors, Evangelists and Voluntary Workers to train and inspire them with the great mission of the Church, which is evangelism?

Signature: Designation Denomination

May I request you to kindly reply on this sheet and send it to Dr. W. D. Coleman, at the address below and he will mail it to me, or you may send it to my address on the top, by air. Dr. W. D. Coleman, Principal A. C. T. C. Luthergiri, Rajahmundry 1, Andhra Pradesh.

Thank you.

Yours sincerely,

B. V. Subbamma

B. V. Subbamma.

P.S.
Even if you do not have all the information, please send what is available—since I need it soon.

Appendix C

QUESTIONNAIRE

1. Is it Scriptural to start separate churches (worship places) for caste converts?

2. Is it helpful for church growth to train pastors and other leaders from caste converts to work among them?

3. Do we make the necessary cultural changes among these converts even at the displeasure of the present church?

4. If the present A. E. L. Church is not willing to evangelize caste people and do the needful, what are the possibilities of church growth, especially among Hindus?

NAME: Mission Field:

Appendix D

Proposed Research Project in Andhra Pradesh

Objectives:

1. To discover the true situation at present with respect to growth, religious affiliation, demographic factors, etc.
2. To find out the actual responsiveness to Christianity of different homogeneous groups.
3. To evaluate the present methods of evangelism.
4. Constructive evaluation of the theological education.
5. To discover the main obstacles for Hindus to become Christians.
6. To be able to find out the ways and means to disciple the Hindu community and to establish churches in their midst.

Research Design.

I. Review of the Literature regarding:

1. History of Andhra Pradesh and its people
2. Anthropological and ethnological descriptions
3. Political history and description of system of government
4. Sociological description
5. Geographical and economic description
6. Religious description
7. The Christian Churches

II. Survey of Non-Christian Religions in Andhra
1. Different religions
2. Different branches of Hindus
3. The philosophy of Hinduism
4. The practices of Hinduism
5. Modern religious movements

III. Survey of the Christian Churches
1. The protestant Churches
2. The Roman Catholic Church
3. Separatists
4. Hindu-Christian movements

IV. The growth of the Churches over a ten-year period (1960-1970)
1. Biological growth (natural) population increase
2. Growth by conversion

V. Harijan Christians and Converts from the Caste Background
1. Christians from different ethnic groups among Harijans
2. Christians from different castes (main castes)
3. Christians from sub-castes
4. Christians from tribal groups

VI. Survey of Christian Outreach to Non-Christians
1. Evangelism in the parishes
2. Bible Women's work
3. Evangelistic campaigns run by a single denomination.
4. Ecumenical campaigns (several denominations)
5. Ashrams
6. Retreat centres
7. Study Centres
8. Urban outreach

VII. Survey of Conversion and Responsiveness
1. How many conversions a year are taking place today?
2. What kind of people?
3. How are they converted?
4. Do they now attend Sunday Service? Where?

5. How often so they have communion?
6. Does the parish pastor visit them? How often?

VIII. Survey of the Available Literature on Evangelism and Church Growth
1. With the pastors and other evangelistic workers
2. In Christian reading rooms
3. In seminary and Bible institutes

IX. Evaluation of Theological Education
1. Different levels of training
2. Curriculum
3. Subjects relating to methods of evangelism
4. Practical work
5. Types of workers trained
6. The relationship of the institution to the Church
7. The relationship with the non-Christian community
8. Future plans

X. Discussion and Interpretation on the Data Collected
1. With responsible members of the Churches (Heads)
2. With some pastors
3. Persons in charge of evangelistic work
4. Other interested persons

XI Personnel and Budget
1. Investigator
2. Research assistant
3. Part-time informants

   Time---two-year period

   The investigator and the research assistant should be assigned full-time to the project for at least six months.

Budget

1. Questionnaires (five different ones) (Duplicating and typing etc.)	Rs. 500.00
2. Postage (100 questionnaires, letters etc.)	700.00
3. Travel for the investigator and the research assistant	1500.00
4. Board and lodging for the investigator	1000.00

and the assistant	
5. Special discussion groups and conferences convened at the Research Centre	700.00
6. Publishing the findings	1200.00
7. Expenses for the informants	500.00
8. Establishment of the Rearch Centre at some existing institution	300.00
total	Rs 6400.00

XII. Final Report

After the research is completed, a full report will be sent to the Churches and Bodies concerned and to other interested parties.

XIII. Application

The findings will be made use of as guiding principles in discipling Hindus.

Appendix E

The Joint Family

Description: Sons of a given pair of parents together with their wives and children, and aged dependents live together in one household. This is the traditional pattern for village India. Though it is changing, it is still the most dominant family pattern.

1. Role of leader: The leader of the joint family is usually the older brother, or the father of the family if he is still active. The leader is responsible for managing all economic affairs. He arranges marriages, controls discipline of the family, delegates work, and is looked to for leadership and moral example by his brothers and all their children. Great burden of responsibility is that of the eldest male, making him virtually a slave to his ascribed position. (Murphy p.30).

2. Younger brothers have to do what is pleasing to the older brother rather than what is pleasing to the wives, supporting him whether he is right or wrong. This results in complete

obedience though they lack independence and incentive.

3. Mother: The oldest brother's mother will be the leader of the household as long as she is active. She dominates the women, demands their obedience, delegates their work. She has been called the 'dictator of the family courtyard' (Charlotte Wiser's book Behind Mud Walls). Since her oldest son respects her and is duty bound to protect her, her position is indisputable and she can greatly influence the entire family through him.

4. Younger brothers' wives: double submission 1. to the husband. 2. to the mother-in-law. There is an element of fear of their husbands for they may be disciplined and punished by them. They must do as the mother-in-law says and even though they may argue and complain they will finally obey.

The best defence these younger wives have is to be very obedient and respectful and thereby win the appreciation of their husbands and elders.

In case of trouble their best defence is to go to their father's or older brother's house for a visit and then stay there indefinitely. This forces the husband's joint family to consider her value, promise her better treatment, and give her gifts etc., and persuade her to return.

A wife generally has three different phases of status:

(a) When she first comes to the household she has very little to do and is expected to learn and adjust to others demands.

(b) When she becomes a mother, her status rises especially if a son is born. She is given more consideration and treated with more equality.

(c) If a son or husband dies, she loses much status, as such tragedies are more or less blamed, traditionally, on the shortcomings of the wife.

5. Children: These are the most privileged of all. Neither responsibility nor submission is required of them. Children get what they want and are generally spoiled until they have to go to work (as the boys do at the age of 10-12), or until they are ready for marriage. They are breast fed for years and carried around long after they can walk, because they wish it. They eat and get what they want. Boys are much more spoiled than girls.

BIBLIOGRAPHY

AIYAPPAN, A.
1965 Social Revolution in a Kerala Village. New York, Asia Publishing House.

ALLEN, Roland
1962 Missionary Methods, St. Paul's or Ours. Grand Rapids, Michigan, William B. Eerdmans Publishing Company.

ANDERSON, Rufus
1967 To Advance the Gospel. Grand Rapids, Michigan, William B. Eerdmans Publishing Company.

ASCHOFF, Theo
1970 Letter to the author, January 14.

BAAGO, Kaj
1968 The Movement Around Subbarao. Bangalore, India, The Christian Literature Society and the Christian Institute for the Study of Religion and Society.

BARNETT, H. G.
1953 Innovation: The Basis of Cultural Change. New York, McGraw-Hill Book Company.

BARRETT, David B.
1968 Schism and Renewal in Africa. London, Oxford University Press.

BAVINCK, J. H.

1948 The Impact of Christianity on the Non-Christian World. Grand Rapids, Michigan, William B. Eerdmans Publishing Company.

1964 An Introduction to the Science of Missions. Philadelphia, Pennsylvania, The Presbyterian and Reformed Publishing Company. (Translated by David Hugh Freeman.)

1966 The Church Between Temple and Mosque: A Study of the Relationship Between the Christian Faith and Other Religions. Grand Rapids, Michigan, William B. Eerdmans Publishing Company.

BEACH, Harlan P.

1908 India and Christian Opportunity. New York, The Student Volunteer Movement for Foreign Missions.

BEALS, R. Alan

1965 Gopalpur: A South Indian Village. New York, Holt, Rinehart and Winston, Publishers.

BENEDICT, Ruth

1934 Patterns of Culture. Boston, Houghton Mifflin Company.

BENNETT, Charles

1968 Tinder in Tabasco. Grand Rapids, Michigan, William B. Eerdmans Publishing Company.

BETEILLE, Andre

1965 Caste, Class, and Power. Berkeley, University of California Press.

BRADSHAW, Malcolm R.

1969 Church Growth Through Evangelism-in-Depth. South Pasadena, California, the William Carey Library.

BROW, Robert
1968 The Church. An Organic Picture of Its Life and Mission. Grand Rapids, Michigan, William B. Eerdmans Publishing Company.

BURCE, Willard
1955 Our New Guinea Mission During Its First Seven Years. Issued at Wabag, New Guinea. Church Report Papers.

BUTTERFIELD, Kenyon L.
1930 The Christian Mission in Rural India. New York and London, International Missionary Council.

CAMPBELL, Alexander
1958 The Heart of India. New York, Alfred A. Knopf Company.

CHURCH OF SOUTH INDIA
1963 Renewal and Advance. Madras, the Church of South India.

DASAGUPTA, S. N.
1927 Hindu Mysticism. Chicago and London, Open Court Publishing Company.

D'EPINAY, Christian-Lalive
1967 "The Training of Pastors and Theological Education." International Review of Missions, 56: 185-192.

DEVANANDAN, P. D.
1960 Christian Participation in Nation-Building. Nagpur, the National Christian Council of India and Bangalore, Christian Institute for the Study of Religion and Society.

DEVANESEN, Chandran
1954 The Cross is Lifted. New York: Friendship Press.

DEVASSY, M.K.
1964 Census of India 1961, Volume VII. Delhi, India, Manager of Publications.

DAVIES, William David
1962 Christian Origin and Judaism. Philadelpia, Westminister Press.

DOLBEER, Martin Luther, Jr.
1959 A History of Lutheranism in Andhra Desa, 1842-1920, (the Telugu Territory of India). New York, United Lutheran Church of America, Board of Foreign Missions.

DRACH, George and KUDER, Calvin F.
1914 The Telugu Mission of the General Council of the Evangelical Lutheran Church in North America. Philadelphia, General Council Publication House.

DUBE, Shyama Charan
1955 Indian Village. New York, Cornell University Press. (Foreword by Morris Edward Opler)

DURNBAUGH, D. F.
1968 The Believer's Church: the History and Character of Radical Protestantism. New York, the Macmillan Company.

ENYART, Paul N.
1970 Interview with the author, February 10.

ESTBORN, S.
1959 Our Village Christians. Madras, The Christian Literature Society.

FILLIOZAT, Jean
1962 India: The Country and Its Traditions. Switzerland, George G. Harper and Company, Ltd. Publishers.

FILSON, Floyd V.
1939 "The Significance of the Early House Churches," Journal of Biblical Literature, 58.

GAMALIEL, James Canjanam
1967 "The Church in Kerala: A People Movement Study." An unpublished thesis, School of World Mission, the Fuller Theological Seminary, Pasadena, California.

GERBER, Vergil
1969 "A New Testament Blueprint: Starting and Organizing Local Churches Overseas." the Evangelical Missions Quarterly, (Fall): 28-37

1970 Interview with the author, February 24.

GIBBARD, Mark
1965 Unity is not Enough. London, A.R. Mowbray and Company, Ltd. Publishers.

GRANT, John Webster
1959 God's People in India. Toronto, The Ryerson Press.

GRAUL, K.
1851 Caste Question. Madras, India, printed at the Athenaeum Press.

GRIFFITHS, Sir Percival
1965 Modern India. New York, Frederick A. Praeger Publishers.

HASTINGS, Adrian
1967 Church and Mission in Modern Africa. New York, Fordham University Press.

HEIMSATH, Charles H.
1964 Indian Nationalism and Hindu Social Reform. New Jersey, Princeton University Press.

HENNEBERGER, James E.

1968 "Ministerial Training in the I. E. L. U." Term Paper Fuller Theological Seminary, Pasadena, California.

HILL, James E.

1969 "Theological Education for the Church in Mission: A Case History of the Baptist, Methodist, and Free Brethren Churches in the Argentine Republic." An unpublished thesis, School of World Mission, Fuller Theological Seminary, Pasadena.

HODGES, Melvin L.

1953 The Indigenous Church. Springfield, Missouri, Gospel Publishing House.

HOGG, A. G.

1947 The Christian Message to the Hindu. London, S.C.M. Press.

HOLLIS, Michael

1962 Paternalism and the Church. New York, Oxford University Press.

HORNER, Norman A., editor.

1968 Protestant Cross Currents in Mission. Nashville, Tennessee, Abingdon Press.

HUTTON, J. H.

1963 Caste in India. New York, Oxford University Press.

KARVE, Irawati

1961 Hindu Society. Poona, India, Deccan College.

KINSLER, F. Ross

1967 An Extension Seminary in Guatemala. Church Growth Bulletin, Vol. 3: 6:10-12.

KRAEMER, Hendrik
1938 The Christian Message in a Non-Christian World. New York, Harper and Brothers.

1956 The Communication of the Christian Faith. Philadelphia, Westminster Press.

1958 A Theology of the Laity. Philadelphia, Westminster Press.

KRAFT, Charles H.
1963 "Christian Conversion or Cultural Conversion." Practical Anthropology, (July-August): 179-187.

KUNG, Hans
1967 The Church. New York, Sheed and Ward.

KURIEN, C. T.
1966 Our Five Year Plans. Bangalore, the Christian Institute for the Study of Religion and Society.

LAMB, Beatrice Pitney
1964 India: A World in Transition. New York, Frederick A. Praeger, Publishers.

LEACH, E. R.
1962 Aspects of Caste in South India, Ceylon, and Northwest Pakistan. Cambridge, published for the Department of Archaeology and Anthropology at the University Press.

LEFEVER, Henry
1968 The Responsible Church and the Foreign Mission. Grand Rapids, Michigan, William B. Eerdmans Publishing Company.

LEHMANN, Arno
1956 It Began at Tranquebar. India, The Christian Literature Society in India. (Translated from the German by M. J. Lutz.)

LINDSELL, Harold, editor.
1966 The Church's Worldwide Mission. Waco, Texas, Word Books.

LUKE, P. Y. and CARMAN, John B.
1968 Village Christians and Hindu Culture. London, Lutterworth Press.

LUTHERA, Veda Prakash
1964 The Secular State and India. London, Oxford University Press.

LUZBETAK, Louis J.
1963 The Church and Culture. Techny, Illinois, the Divine Word Publications.

MADRAS CHRISTIAN COLLEGE
1967 India Today. Bangalore, the Christian Institute for the Study of Religion and Society, and the Christian Literature Society.

MADSEN, W. Westergaard (Bishop)
1970 Letter to the author, February 23.

MAJUMDAR, D. N.
1962 Caste and Communication in an Indian Village. Bombay, Asia Publishing House.

MANGUM, John
1968 "New Fields." A study for presentation to the Board of World Missions, Lutheran Church in America.

MANIKAM, Rajah B.
1954 Christianity and the Asian Revolution. Printed in the United States of America.

MARRIOT, McKim
1960 Caste Ranking and Community Structure in Five Regions of India and Pakistan, Poona, Deccan College.

MARRIOT, McKim, editor.
1955 Village India. Chicago, The University of Chicago Press.

MAYER, Adrian C.
1960 Caste and Kinship in Central India. California, The University of California Press.

McGAVRAN, Donald A.
1955 Bridges of God. New York, Friendship Press

1957 How Churches Grow. New York, Friendship Press.

1965 Church Growth and Christian Mission. New York, Harper and Row Publishers.

1970 Understanding Church Growth. Grand Rapids, Michigan, William B. Eerdmans Publishing Company.

McGAVRAN, Donald A., editor.
1969 Church Growth Bulletin. Volumes I-VI.

1970 Church Growth Bulletin. January, 1970.

MEISSNER, Miss M.
1969 Interview held with the author, December 18.

MICHENER, James
1969 "Those Fabulous Italian Designers," in The Reader's Digest (September): 157-166.

MISRA, B. B.
1961 The Indian Middle Classes: Their Growth in Modern Times. London, Oxford University Press.

MOFFETT, Samuel H. (Lecture)
n.d. "The Biblical Bakcground of Evangelism."

NAIR, Kusum
1961 Blossoms in the Dust. New York, Frederick A. Praeger, Publishers.

NATIONAL CHRISTIAN COUNCIL
1966 Findings of the National Consultation on the Mission of the Church in Contemporary India Held at Nasrapur, India. The Wesley Press, Mysore, India.

NEHRU, B. K.
Speaking of India. Washington, D.C., Information Service of India.

NEILL, Stephen
1966 A History of Christian Missions. London, Penguin Books. (Grand Rapids, Michigan, Wm. B. Eerdmans Publishing Company.

NEUDOERFFER, J. F.
1968 "Proposals and Patterns of Relationships." Paper (printed) read at the Andhra Evangelical Lutheran Church Long Range Planning Conference, October 14-23, 1968, at Bhimavaram, Andhra, India.

NEVIUS, John L.
1958 The Planting and Development of Missionary Churches. Philadelphia, Pennsylvania, The Presbyterian and Reformed Publishing Company.

NEWBIGIN, Lesslie
1960 The Mission and Unity of the Church. South Africa, Rhodes University.

1960 "Mission and Missions," Christianity Today, (August): 23.

1969 The Finality of Christ. Richmond, Virginia, John Knox Press.

NIDA, Eugene A.
1960 Message and Mission. New York, Harper and Row Publishers.

NILES, D. T.
1962 Upon the Earth. Madras, Christian Literature Society.

OLSON, Gilbert W.
1969 Church Growth in Sierra Leone. Grand Rapids, Michigan, William B. Eerdmans Publishing Company.

ORR, J. Edwin
1970 Evangelical Awakenings in India. 70 Janpath, New Delhi, Masihi Sahitya Sanstha.

ORR, Robert A.
1970 Interview with the author, February 26.

PANIKAR, K. M.
1963 The Foundation of New India. London, George, Allen and Unwin, Ltd.

PATON, David M.
1965 New Forms of Ministry. London, Edinburgh House Press.

PAUL, Rajaiah D.
1952 The Cross Over India. London, S.C.M. Press,

PAULSON, Ernie
1970 Interview with author, January 30, February 8

PETHYRIDGE,
n.d. Pamphlet. Published in the United States of America.

PHILLIPS, Godfrey
1936 The Untouchable's Quest. New York, Friendship Press.

PICKETT, J. W.
1933 Christian Mass Movements in India. Lucknow, Lucknow Publishing House.

1938 Christ's Way to India's Heart. Lucknow, Lucknow Publishing House.

PICKETT, J. W., McGAVRAN, D.A., and SINGH, G. H.
1962 Church Growth and Group Conversion. Lucknow, Lucknow Publishing House.

POTHACAMURY, Thomas
1958 The Church in Independent India. Maryknoll, New York, Maryknoll Publications (World Horizon Reports).

RAGHAVAN, D., editor.
1961 Farmers of India. Vol II. New Delhi, Indian Council of Agricultural Research.

RAJARATNAM, K.
1970 The Structure of the Church/Congregation in the Indian Setting; Their Factors. Felci, India, Ad Hoc Study Committee.

RAMBO, David Lloyd
1968 "Training Competent Leaders for the Christian and Missionary Alliance Churches of the Philippines."
An unpublished thesis, Fuller Theological Seminary. Pasadena, California.

READ, William R.
1965 New Patterns of Church Growth in Brazil. Grand Rapids, Michigan, William B. Eerdmans Publishing Company.

REDFIELD, Robert
1967 The Little Community, Peasant Society and Culture. Chicago, University of Chicago Press.

RICHARDSON, William J.
1966 Revolution in Missionary Thinking. Maryknoll, New York, Maryknoll Publications.

ROSS, Byron W.
n. d. Training Lay Workers. New York, The Christian and Misssionary Alliance.

SAMBAYYA, E.
1969 Letter to the author, December 30.

SAVAGE, Peter
1969 "A Bold Move for More Realistic Theological Training," Evangelical Missions Quarterly, (Winter): 65-73.

SCANLON, A. Clark
1962 Church Growth Through Theological Education (In Guatemala). Guatemala, El Faro.

SCHMITTHENNER, S. W.
1968 "The Structure and Outreach of the Andhra Evangelical Lutheran Church in Rural Andhra." Paper (printed) submitted at the Andhra Evangelical Lutheran Church Long Range Planning Conference, October 14-23,,1968 in Andhra.

SEAMANDS, John T.
1964 The Supreme Task of the Church. Grand Rapids, Michigan, William B. Eerdmans Publishing Company.

1966 "What McGavran's Church Growth Thesis Means," Evangelical Missions Quarterly, (Fall): 21-31.

SHEARER, Roy E.
1966 Wildfire: Church Growth in Korea. Grand Rapids, Michigan, William B. Eerdmans Publishing Company.

SIEBERT, Eva Maria
1970 Letter to the author, January 6.

SMALLEY, William A., editor.
1967 Readings in Missionary Anthropology. Tarrytown, New York, Practical Anthropology, Inc.

SPRUTH, Erwin L.
1960 "The Administration of the Sacraments in the Enga Church." Paper prepared for the Staff Conference of New Guinea Lutheran Mission.

SRINIVAS, M. N.
1967 Social Change in Modern India. California, University of California Press.

SRINIVAS, M. N., editor.
1960 India's Villages. Bombay, Asia Publishing House.

STREETER, B. H.
1921 The Message of Sadhu Sundar Singh. New York, The Macmillan Company.

SUBBAMMA, B. V.
1968 "Mission of the Church in Andhra Pradesh." An unpublished B.D. thesis, Serampore University, near Calcutta, India.

SWANSON, Allen John
1968 "A Comparative Study of Independent and Mainline Churches in Taiwan." An unpublished thesis, Fuller Theological Seminary, Pasadena.

SWANSON, Miss R. H.
1969 Interview held with author, December 19.

TAKAMI, Toshihiro
1969 "Concepts of Ledership and Their Meaning for for Growth of Christian Churches." An unpublished thesis, Fuller Theological Seminary.

TAYLOR, Richard W.
1963 Mud Walls and Steel Mills. New York, Friendship Press.

THOMAS, M. M., and CHANDRAN, J. R.
1956 Religious Freedom. Bangalore, The Committee for Literature on Social Concerns.

THOMS, Paul
1963 The Theology of Chakka Rai. Bangalore, The Christian Institute for the Study of Religion and Society.

TILAK, L.
1956 From Brahn a to Christ. London, United Society for Christian Literature, Lutterworth Press.

TILL, Barry, editor.
1965 Changing Frontiers in the Mission of the Church. London, S.P.C.K.

TIPPETT, A.R.
1967 "Religious, Group Conversion in Non-Western Society." Research-in-progress Pamphlet Series, Number 11.

1969 Verdict Theology in Missionary Theory. Lincoln, Illinois, Lincoln Christian College Press.

VICEDOM, G.F.
1961 Church and People in New Guinea. London, United Society for Christian Literature, Lutterworth Press.

VIDYARTHI, L.P.
1967 Leadership in India. Bombay, Asia Publishing House.

VIGUS, John A.
1970 Interview with author, January 24.

WAGNER, P.
1970 Interview with the author, February 5.

WEBER, H. R.
1957 The Communication of the Gospel to Illiterates. London, S.C.M. Press, Ltd.

WEBSTER, Douglas
1964 Patterns of Part-Time Ministry. Great Britain, World Dominion Press.

WINTER, Ralph D., editor.
1969 Theological Education by Extension. William Carey Library, South Pasadena, California.

WOLD, Joseph Conrad
1968 God's Impatience in Liberia. Grand Rapids, Michigan, William B. Eerdmans Publishing Company.

WOLF, Thomas A.
n.d. "The Structure of the Church and the Ministry of the Church in the New Testament." Term Paper, Fuller Theological Seminary.

WORLD COUNCIL OF CHURCHES
1968 "The Church for Others and The Church for the World." Geneva, World Council of Churches.

WORLD HORIZON REPORT
1958 Report No. 20. Digest of Catholic Missionary History. Maryknoll, New York, Maryknoll Publications.

WRIGHT, Kenyon E.
n.d. A Mission of Peace to An Age of Change. India, The Northeast India Ecumenical Social and Industrial Institute.

WORLDWIDE EVANGELIZATION CRUSADE
1961 Review of Mission Fields. London.

ZINKIN, Taya
1962 Caste Today. London, Oxford University Press.

1965 India. New York, Walker and Company.

1966. Challenges in India. London, Chatto and Windus.

INDEX

Aiyappan, Dr. A., 7
Ambedkar, Dr., 5
Andhra, 4, 61, 91, 94
  churches largely Harijan, 64
  theological education in, 133-134
Andhra Christian Theological College, 30, 121, 132-133, 136, 153
Andhra Evangelical Lutheran Church, 18, 19, 91
  ashrams in, 38
  indigenous movements in, 128-130
  people movements in, 107
  survey of evangelism among Hindus, 42-51
Andhra Pradesh, 3, 13, 59, 74, 86, 101
  population of, 119
Ashram, 2, 38-41, 82-83, 87, 112, 133, 137, 152, 160
Azariah, Bishop, 156

Baago, Dr. Kaj, 95-97
Baptist Church, Canadian, 16-18
Baptist Churches, Samevasam of Telegu, 20-22
Barth, Karl, 159
Batto (beauty mark), 163
Bhajana (special worship service), 39-40, 81-82
Bible Training School, Charlotte Swenson Memorial, 38-39, 120
Bible women, 45, 47, 50
Board of World Missions of the Lutheran Church in America, 1, 148-149, 151, 156, 165
Brotherhood, 86, 99

Caste, 4, 6-11, 43, 45, 53, 112
Caste converts, 74, 92, 116, 150
  extension training needed for, 155
  priest should live with, 126
  responsive, 123
Catechumenate, 135
Charlotte Swenson Memorial Bible Training School, *See Bible Training School*
Church, 51-52, 68-79, 79, 86
  apostolic, 55
  foreignness of, 56
  form of, 127-128
  introverted, 145
  mission of, 62-66
  opportunity to evangelize Sudhras, 43
  Protestant groups in Andhra, 13
  unity of, 91
  witnessing, 100
Church Growth, 2, 61-2, 149
  emphasis on church planting, 69
  keys to in cities, 122-123
  new patterns of, Ch. 5, 100-124
  training needed, 136-137
Church of South India, 13
Church planting, 119, 162
  the goal, 69
  needed among Middle Classes, 123, 131
  Paul's example of, 73
  trained leaders needed for, 121, 153-155
Coleman, Dr. W.D. 133
Communication, 109, 118-119
Congregation, 43, 77, 94
Constitution, India's, 6, 7, 51, 52
Conversion, 37, 49, 52, 69, 74, 93-9
  author's personal experience of, 25-33
  misunderstood as shift to another group, 76
  outreach of convert women, 46

statement on by National Consultation, 53-54
Cross, offence of, 52, 74
Culture, 55, 163-164

Davies, W.D., 127

Ethnic group, 29, 79
Evangelism, 146-147
  Bible the basic tool for, 161
  difficulties, 74
  every convert a potential for, 37, 49
  industrial, 120
  new patterns of, 1, 100-101, 144, 151, 159-160
  in the New Testament mold, 67-68, 71
  technical expertness needed for, 144

Face-to-Face Society, 109

Gerber, Vergil, 68, 70-71
Gospel, 1, 32, 39, 43, 50, 54, 67, 84, 100, 131
Guatemala Plan (of leadership training), 139-141
Guru, 25, 32, 113-114
  Christ as Guru, 78
  indigenous gurus, 128-130
Gurukul Theological College, 132, 153
Gutmann, Bruno, 59

Harijans
  Andhra Evangelical Church based on, 42, 44, 60, 119
  caste people feel Christianity belongs to, 27, 29-32, 35-37, 41, 78, 95
  caste people must have separate churches from, 48, 83, 85-87, 107-108
  churches static, 24, 64
  church must no longer be limited to, 51
  Hindus require different approach from, 113
  responsible to evangelize their own, 149-150, 164-165
  underprivileged, landless servants, 57
  untouchability abolished by Gandhi, 6
Harvest theology, 104
Hindus, 2, 28, 125
  approach to, 114-117
  caste feeling strong among, 8, 30, 61
  difficult to join Harijan community, 31, 94
  new patterns needed to reach, 1, 50
  pride in religion, 113
  separate congregations needed for, 77-79, 84, 87, 94
  unbiblical barriers to, 52
Hindustani Bible Institute, 132
Hogg, Dr. A.G., 97-98, 112-115, 117
Home communions, 90
Homogeneous groups
  bring to repentance, 61
  discipling by house churches, 79-80
  Gospel must be related to, 34, 59
  conglomerate church self-defeating, 60
  not necessary to join another group, 67, 74, 108
  resistant units, 122
  should each have their leaders, 129-130
House churches, 66, 122, 137, 155
  in Andhra, 81, 88-89
  advantages of, 82-89
  function of, 89-90
  indigenous, 92-94
  Scriptural, 79-81
Hutton, J.H., 7

India, 3, 6, 55, 56
  rapid change in, 101
Indigenous, 56, 128
  literature, 162
  worship, 162
Indigenous church, 110-111
  among caste Hindus, 147
  leadership, 128-130
  principles, 93-94
  Pentecostal in Chile, 141-142
  slavery to principles, 146

Joint family, 6

Kammas, 3, 4, 15, 28-30, 32, 36, 41, 43, 87, 107, 126, 162
  Subbarao Movement, 94-97
Kapus, 3, 4, 15, 36, 41, 43, 107, 162
Karma, 117
Karve, Dr. Iravati, 9

Lay leaders, 22, 65, 149
  need training by extension, 138-140

needed to reach caste people, 88, 93, 152
should be natural leaders, 122
Leadership, 72, 74
apostolic type needed, 127-128
from caste background needed, 125-127, 147
paid leaders, 131, 152
types and levels of, 130, 131
Lutheran Bible Training Institute, 132
Lutheran Church, *See Andhra Evangelical Lutheran Church*
Luther, Martin, 65, 105
Luzbetak, Dr. Louis J., 129-130

Malabar Syrian Christian Church, 58
Mangalmandiram Bible School, 134
Mangum, Dr. John, 2, 64, 103
Mark, Dr. Gibbard, 87, 88
Mass Movements, *See People Movements*
McGavran, Dr. Donald A., 2, 11, 52, 58, 61, 67, 74, 94, 102-103, 122-123, 146
Mission, 53, 56, 61-62, 68, 70-71, 94, 144, 146-147

Neill, Bishop, 145
Newbigin, Bishop, 59, 76-77, 133, 144-145
Newdoerffer, Dr. J.F., 2, 148-149
Nida, Dr. Eugene A., 57, 109
Niles, Dr. D.T. 62, 102

Order for women, 158
Ordination, 156
for women, 157-158
Outcaste, *See Harijan*

Panchayat (village council), 40
People Movements, 11, 24, 34, 42, 105-107
Pickett, J.W., 2, 33-34, 36-37, 57, 103, 111
Population explosion, 118
Prayer cells, 83-84

Rajaratnam, Dr. K., 98
Rama, 26
Ramapatnam Theological Seminary, 132
Reddys, 3, 4, 36, 43, 107, 126, 162
Repentance, 52
Retreat Training Centre, 132

Sanskrit, 5
Schmitthenner, Rev. S.W., 2, 42-44 47-49, 77-78, 126, 151
Scripture distribution, 161
Singapore Bible College, 153-154
Singh, Bakht, 13
Smalley, Dr. William A., 56
South Andhra Lutheran Church, 22
Spruth, Rev. Erwin L., 134-136
Subbarao Movement among Kammas, 94-97
Sudras, 5, 33-35, 43-49, 57, 126
priesthood of believers among, 8
special parishes for, 77-78, 85
training of, 136

Tent-makers, 23, 137-138
Telegu, 4, 17
Theological education, 132-134, 138, 154
extension training needed in Andhra, 142-143, 154-155
Guatemala Plan of extension training, 139-141
Theology of Search, 67, 68
Thomas, Dr. M.M., 95-96
Tilak, Narayan Vaman, 74-75, 116
Tippett, Dr. A.R., 106-107, 110-11 155
Transmigration, 115
Trueblood, Dr. Elton, 69-70, 72-74

Unpaid leaders, 14, 23, 152
Urban churches, 119, 121

Winter, Dr. Ralph D., 139-141, 160
Women, outreach of, 36-37, 46, 126
Bible schools for, 134
World Council of Churches, 92
Worship, Indian pattern of, 111-11

ABOUT THE AUTHOR

Miss B. V. Subbamma was born in a Hindu family in Andhra Pradesh, South India. She became a Christian while a student at Andhra Christian College, where she obtained her B.A. in 1947. She subsequently received a Bachelor of Education from Andhra University, a Master of Arts from New York University, a Bachelor of Divinity from Serampore University, and a Master of Arts in Missions from Fuller Theological Seminary. The New York University chapter of Alpha Kappa Delta, the international honor society in socioloty, showed its recognition of her ability to do research by electing her to its membership in 1958.

Miss Subbamma is the principal of the Charlotte Swenson Memorial Bible Training School. Because of her background, she feels a special call to evangelize Hindus, and conducts gospel meetings in public places where thousands of Hindu men and women gather. She has addressed audiences of thirty to forty thousand at the Andhra Christian Convention. Many were reached with the Gospel through the Ashram at Rajahmundry, which she designed and supervised. Few are as well qualified as she to speak of methods of evangelizing Hindus.

Printed in U.S.A. by Church Press

Printed in the United States
1087200002B/181-240